Accidental Cowgirl

A City Slicker's Life On an Eastern Oregon Ranch

Kristy St. Clair

Kristy St. Clair
enjoy!

PHOTOGRAPHS AND IMAGES

INTERIOR PAGES

First photograph page;

Phil and Kristy at the cabin on Poison Creek in Izee

(top) by Phil St. Clair (bottom) by Jim Shields

Second photo page;

Ranch and house in Izee

(both photographs by Phil St. Clair)

Image page;

Map copyright © 2007 by Bear Creek Press of Wallowa, Oregon

Izee Brands by Phil St. Clair

FRONT COVER

Kristy St. Clair, 1998

(photograph by Phil St. Clair)

BACK COVER

Drainage of the South Fork of the John Day River on the St. Clair Ranch in Izee, Oregon

(photograph copyright © by Bear Creek Press)

Inset: author Kristy St. Clair and her Border Collie, Dollie

(photograph by Phil St. Clair)

PRINTING HISTORY

A version of the chapter "Buckaroo Wisdom" appeared in RANGE Magazine, spring 2004

Bear Creek Press First Edition: April 2007

Printed in the United States of America

ISBN: 978-1-930111-68-4

Contents

Dedication

With love, I dedicate this book to Phil. Friend and husband, in that order. To my mom and dad and to Phil's parents all of who made ranch life possible. And to the precious ones who are gone save a place for me at the ranch above.

Acknowledgements

Thanks to my editor, Mark Highberger, who had no idea what he was getting into when he took me on. A patient teacher he never settled for mediocre writing. Like a cowdog, he nipped at my heels to keep me moving and, like Jeff Gallagher, he threw me a loop when I was stuck or pulled me in when I rambled on in confusion.

Specifically, thank you to the Izee ranchers, past and present: the Keerins, Officers, Hydes, Rickmans, Schnabeles, Bedorthas, Martins, Swindlehursts, Browns, Rodgers, Wegners, Nelsons, Dianne Matheson, Bidwells, Andersons, and Hodges. I pray this book reveals the respect and admiration I have for your intelligence, work ethic, and generosity of spirit. Please accept my gratitude for allowing us to hang around all of you soaking up your knowledge. Thanks for your help on frigid nights, for taking our phone calls during cow emergencies, and for inviting us to family gatherings making us a part of the community.

Also, thanks to friends on the fringes: the Cernazanus, Moores, Southwoths, Cronins, Stinnetts, Zinns, Robertsons, Kasey Nash, Tom Winters, Tom Hunt, Ted and Skylar, Traftons, Aasnesses, Lemons, Hollidays, Olivers, Barkers, Galbreaths, Hueckmans, Taylors, Cernys, Gilmores, Paladijczuks, Wilkinsons, Thompsons, Ken Delano, everyone at the Soil and Water Conservation office, Dixie Lund, Dave Traylor and Hugh Farrell, Neals, Unterwegners, and the "boys" Tom and Andy. If I left anyone out, chalk it up to early dementia. And a special thanks to Billie Bird, wherever you are.

Thanks to our families for their eager companionship, help and support through the years. The ranch supplied the background for loads of memories. Love to all of you.

Finally, to the three funsters, Phil, Wade, and Jim Shields, who were with me, making everything worthwhile.

Then (above) and now (right):
Kristy and Phil St. Clair at the cabin
on Poison Creek in Izee.

Ranch and house in Izee, 1973

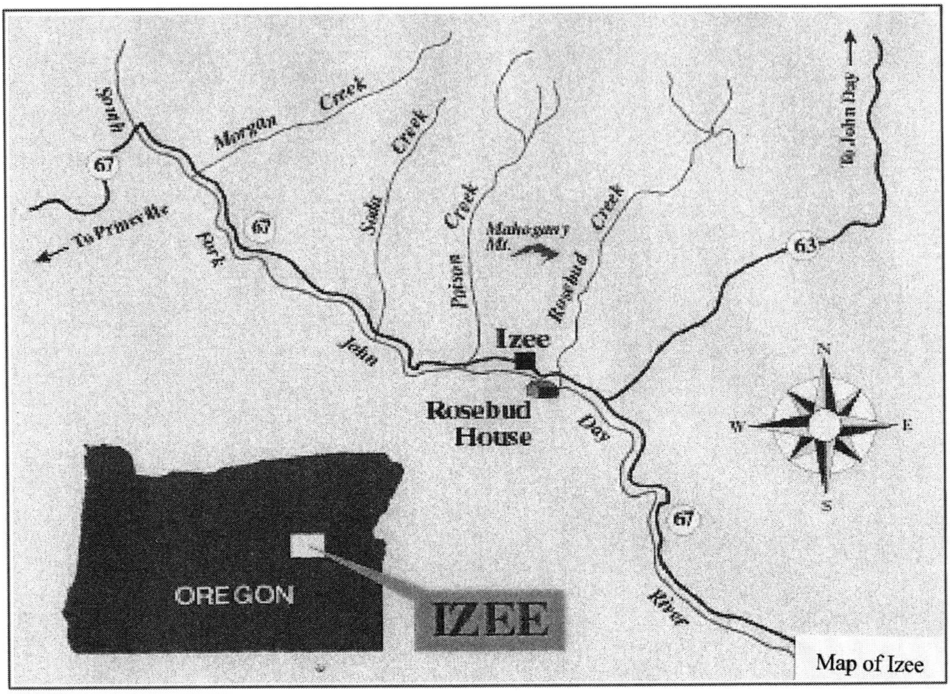

Map of Izee

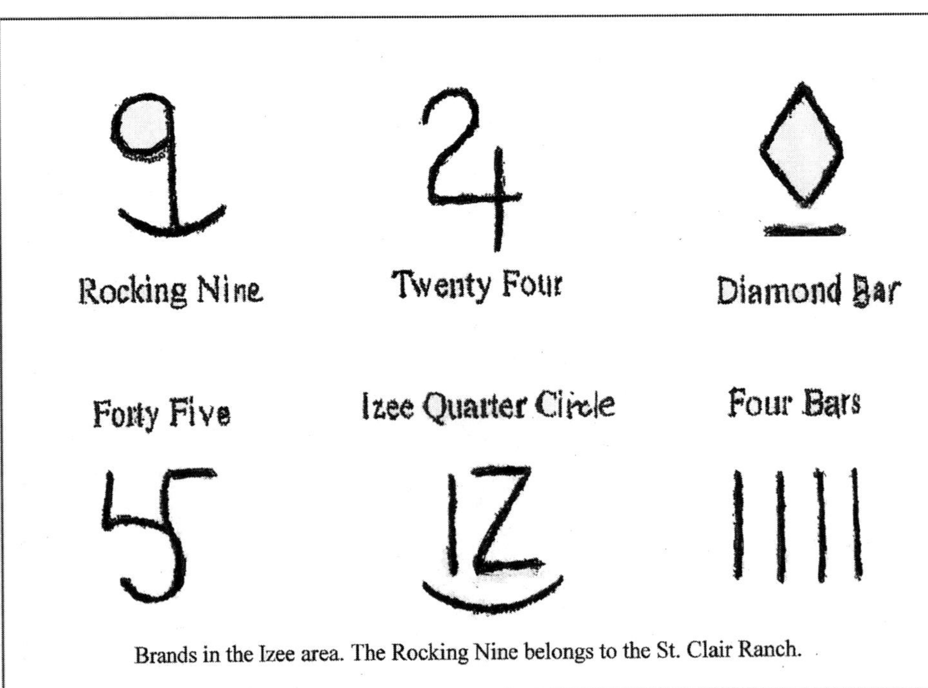

Brands in the Izee area. The Rocking Nine belongs to the St. Clair Ranch.

Dad's Ranch

In the fall of 1973, we wound our way out of the green-carpeted Willamette Valley of western Oregon, crested the snow-capped Cascades, and drove onward, toward the new life waiting for us in eastern Oregon. Although I didn't know it at the time, this was to be a journey that carried me by chance, luck, fate, circumstance—or whatever you want to call it, but I always think of it as an accident—from city slicker to cowgirl.

During our drive east, my mother, Dart, steered her little Toyota as I watched the lush forests and high mountains transform abruptly to low rolling hills dotted with juniper trees. My husband, Phil, slept in the backseat, but the pungent aromas of the east side of the mountains soon woke him. He sat up, sniffing the air. "What an incredible smell!"

It was the first thing we noticed. Like a well-perfumed fourth passenger inside the car, the scent of the high desert joined our traveling party. Behind us, back home in Portland, lay the mass of people, cars, and buildings smelling of the chemical blend that happens only when humanity crushes together.

The second thing we noticed as we followed the long, steep mountain into the sleepy town of Warm Springs was that people weren't hurrying as they did in the big city. Here old and young alike lounged against storefronts and strolled along the streets. The houses were few and far from one another. It was the same with Madras and Prineville.

I prayed this fresh country with its dry, grassy fields and rocky mesas marked the end of our long quest for space and privacy. I dreamed of a house of our own.

The beginnings of that dream came in August at 2:30 in the morning with a telephone call from my dad, Paul Timm. He said he had just bought a cattle ranch in Izee—where in the world was *Izee*?—with a fixer-upper ranch hand's house standing on it and Rosebud Creek running next to it. It didn't bother him that he'd never owned a ranch before; he couldn't pass up a bargain.

"The Rocking Nine Ranch," he said over the phone. "Four thousand acres with cattle already on it. Do you want to move there?"

A few weeks earlier, he'd escaped from the Oregon State Mental Hospital in Salem after going on another of his alcoholic binges and then dashing out of an Oregon City motel—buck naked except for a flimsy robe—across four lanes of fifty-five-mile-an-hour traffic. Seems he'd run out of Jack Daniels and was headed for the liquor store. The motel owners called *me*, his only child. I'd made sure Dad kept my name and address in his wallet for emergencies such as this.

So after I made a reluctant phone call or two to folks who make commitment happen, Dad was whisked away to the state hospital for thirty days. This was his second stay. An absolute optimist, Dad viewed this small interruption in his life as another adventure, as a challenge to conquer. Every time he was committed, as they were fitting him into his first pair of hospital scuffies, he was already planning his escape—but not before he toyed with me a bit for putting him there. The phone calls began immediately.

"Kristy, someone peed in my shoe last night." I heard the mischievous note in his voice. "I'm in *real danger*."

Of course, I knew better. Dad was a big Scandinavian, brought up on lefse and lutefisk, and stood 6-foot 2-inches barefooted. Although he was a lover and not a fighter, people didn't mess with him. And he *always* escaped.

This time, the hospital administrator called to tell me he had no idea where Dad was, and they were sorry that he'd slipped away again.

"I just can't understand it, Mrs. St. Clair," he said. "We have attendants stationed at each exit at all times, and he manages to sneak past them. It's astonishing how resourceful he is."

I knew that already but still felt for the guy. My dad was not a normal patient.

"DAD, WHERE...*ARE*...YOU?" I said when he called me with the news about the ranch, giving him a righteous brew of red-hot anger mixed with desperate worry.

"I'm at Caesar's Palace in Vegas!" he said, laughing, undaunted, and blessed with a father's love and forgiveness for a caring but frothy daughter. "Joey—you remember him? The owner of Caesar's? He called me at the hospital and said Frank Sinatra was his headliner. Okay, maybe I called him. But honey pie, it's *Frank*! I have front row seats! Wally Schirra is sitting next to me. We were talking about flying. Which reminds me, sweetheart, right after the show I'm flying to the ranch. I've called your mother. You can drive there with her. I LOVE YOU." Click.

I *knew* it! Frustration seized me so hard I whacked the phone on our rickety bedside table, causing Phil to explode off his fluffy pillow and yell, "Come on in! The door's open!"

The call was so typical of my dad. The man was a loveable rascal. Bigger than life, he loved as many women as he could get his hands on, and lived off borrowed money with a gusto that would have put Al Capone to shame. His insatiable appetite and childlike enthusiasm infected everyone he knew.

Among his numerous loves, and not in any specific order, were Frank Sinatra, Jack Daniels, flying, my mother, and me. In spite of his philandering ways, he and my mother remained occasional lovers. My parents divorced when I left the nest at eighteen. The split made them even more amorous for each other, if that was possible. When near each other, they were combative. Fueled by a few cocktails, Sinatra singing on the stereo, and a waiting bed, it was a perfect recipe for sexual tension. Their marriage had been equivalent to two trains running full speed towards each other with only sex on their minds.

He started flying when he was twelve and could pilot a plane as easily as buttering his morning toast. As a kid, I was swept up in his madcap antics. Dad favored twin engines, and we flew everywhere. We'd jet off to Hawaii on a lark, yet my underwear would be old and raggedy. Many times while on a "vacation"—eventually I became suspicious of these—we landed at tiny, out-of-the-way airstrips on the outskirts of big cities because creditors were waiting at the big airports to repossess the plane.

Dad always seemed to know where they were and managed to keep one step ahead of them.

When they came after him, he'd already be in the pilot's seat with the engines on full, advising us to hotfoot it into the plane. I became adept at jumping on the wing, hurling myself into the backseat, and buckling up before Mom got the door shut.

In two minutes flat, we'd be bumping and bouncing down the tarmac. Then in the blink of an eye, we were looking straight up at the clouds. When I was still too young to know, I'd ask him, "What's the big hurry, Dad?"

"Oh, we just have to get up in the air before the weather changes, dumpling." he'd say, grinning, secretly tickled that he'd once again slipped from their grasp. He loved the intrigue and the chase.

He also loved a good, juicy business deal. The more elusive the deal, the better he liked it. A wily entrepreneur, he could breeze into a bank and borrow outlandish amounts of cash with no collateral except his quick humor, sharp intelligence, and ballsy attitude. He would find a failing business, locate a buyer for it, and charge the poor sap two or three times the amount of the original purchase price. While gaining the confidence of gullible followers and the respect of wary rivals, he accumulated and lost large fortunes. He accomplished all this repeatedly, after coming off binges that would kill the average man. The ranch was his latest trophy, and he acquired it in typical fashion.

After hearing about the ranch for sale in Izee, he was able to persuade an acquaintance in Alaska to buy it. The fellow came to the ranch during the hardest-working time—haying season—and it didn't take him long to decide he wanted to go back to Alaska. That's when Dad brokered a deal on the ranch by talking a banker into financing him. Later I learned he called the banker on the public phone as a group of mental patients in various states of befuddlement waited in line behind him. He probably convinced them he had some urgent business transaction by offering to buy each of them a Mercedes.

"Your mother's coming to the ranch this weekend," he said, "so why don't you come, too? You can even bring Phil."

I'd been married for four years, and occasionally I'd catch Dad giving me a sad, bewildered look, glancing from me to Phil and back again, as if he just didn't know me anymore because I'd married Phil. It was obvious he worried about my intelligence. To Dad, Phil would always be "four-eyes," the upstart teenager who stole the darling little princess away from her father's castle. Dad and Phil's anti-love affair was a forever thing, so I knew Phil would look forward to the trip about as much as he would jumping into a barrel of diarrhea-plagued slugs.

"Nope. Not a chance." Phil told me the next morning. "Even if a Tsunami were on its way to Portland and we had to beat feet over the Cascades to high ground." He gobbled down a stack of fat blueberry pancakes, then swabbed irritably at the syrup caught in his thick beard. "Not if forty big-breasted, naked women awaited me at the ranch your dad *supposedly* bought. No, no, *no*!"

That evening while Phil was out in our studio working on a piece of sculpture for a Portland gallery, I called my mother to find out about Dad and his new toy, the ranch. She assured me it was the real deal. Mom knew Phil and I wanted to move out of the city, even though we were both city kids. In the back of my mind, I was wondering if this was our chance. The big obstacle was getting involved with my Dad. I told her about Phil's reaction.

"Honey pie, you need to entice him," Mom said. "What is one of Phil's greatest pleasures besides you, baby?"

I racked my brain. What does Phil love? "Beer," I said.

"No, sweetheart. *Fishing*. The Upper South Fork of the John Day River flows through the ranch. Your father told me he's spied some gigantic trout darting out of deep holes, nabbing grasshoppers. He said some of them rivaled steelhead."

So with the call of the river whispering sweet promises in Phil's ears, Mom picked us up the next afternoon. And on a sunny day in late summer, we began our first journey to the ranch and into the land of spat-out chews and Budweiser-beer hangovers. None of us knew the incredible detour our life was about to take.

First Journey

Sardines would have been more comfortable in their can than we were in Mom's Toyota. Phil, conked out again in the backseat, lay among piles of luggage, pillows, Mom's cartons of cigarettes, and a scummy old tackle box with pieces of unidentifiable fish parts stuck to it. He had the tip of a fishing pole wedged under his neck, with a wayward strand of his shoulder-length hair twisted through the line. Although his face squished against the window and a discreet stream of drool wound its way down his cheek, he was smiling. That was a good sign.

We'd been driving for five hours now, and it was pitch black. Stars showed up like tiny yard lights in the sky. Gosh—stars! Where had they been all my life?

We passed through Paulina, a community of about forty people. Mom said the next town was almost a hundred miles farther on, and Izee was about halfway between. What kind of place was this ranch, I wondered, and why weren't any people living out here? The road grew narrower and the drive even slower, seeing as how we almost ran over five deer, three porcupines, and a bobcat. Near Izee, a former post office site named for a cattleman's *IZ* brand, the road became a gravel path.

Izee turned out to be a tiny community located forty-two miles southwest from the nearest town of Canyon City, whose population was just a bit more than seven hundred. The isolated valley surrounding Izee included eight ranches within a twenty-mile radius. The schoolhouse, the teacherage, a cemetery, and a community hall were the pivotal points, and all of them stood on Dad's land.

Finally, we turned left at a wire gate, drove another mile-and-a-half up a dirt road and toward a yard light, and stopped at an old two-story ranch house surrounded by towering silver maples. Dad stood waiting for us in the driveway. I tried to give him my best stern look for all he'd put me through, but he didn't notice. So I hugged him instead. He looked good. His short time at the hospital had put some weight back on his frame.

"I missed you," I told him. "It's incredible here, isn't it?"

"I knew you'd like it!" he said. "Did you know I've hunted this area for years?" I was so tired that I had to make myself look interested. "I've stayed at the Sheehans' ranch when they ran a hunting camp. Angus is sure a character. I think he likes his whiskey a little too much, though." I peeked at Dad and saw he was completely serious.

After hugs and howdies were exchanged all around, Dad led Phil and me up an almost vertical, impossibly narrow stairwell to our rooms. Ever hopeful, he started to show Phil a separate room across the hall before remembering we were married. Mom and Dad, of course, also shared a room.

The next morning, the sun filled our small bedroom. So did the aroma from fried ham, butter-drenched hash browns, and fresh-perked coffee. Dad loved to make a big breakfast. All of a sudden, my appetite was huge; I felt as if I could devour a Cape buffalo.

I swung my legs down from the lumpy but comfortable iron bed and stepped to the window. Our view looked north up the canyon to the edge of the Malheur National Forest, maybe a half-mile away. The ranch house rested between steep hills that snaked along the dirt road we'd traveled last night. At the bottom, where we'd turned off the county road, the meadowed valley ran east-west with the upper South Fork John Day River meandering in a long scribble through the flood plain. This draw, Mom had explained during our trip, was Poison Creek, which had its own little creek flowing south where it joined the river. The scene looked like a western movie set—lopsided corrals, oddly placed fences, an ancient barn, two sway-backed bay horses, and a hodgepodge of different-sized outbuildings. All of it had a friendly, aged quality. The smells, the view—everything was from another era. A spell was cast. I felt enchanted by this place. My gosh, I realized I *loved* this place.

Each direction I looked I fell more in love. I knew in my bones that two young hippie craftsmen—one with long locks and beard and the other with waist-long braids—were about to do the unthinkable, that Phil and I would somehow return to live here on this ranch. I was finally home. But how would Phil react to the fact that at age twenty-three, I'd decided that this is where I wanted to spend the rest of my days?

For over a year, Phil and I had worked in a Portland gallery-shop as apprentice leather craftsmen. The people we met were quirky and stimulating, and we felt lucky to have stumbled into them. But when one of the owners died of cancer, his partner decided to close the shop, so Phil and I opened our own place, operating it for four years. Five years of working to build our reputations in the art world had taken its toll on me. Hunkered at our tables all day, designing and creating our pieces, I ached to toil outside in the dirt, around plants and rocks and animals of all sizes. This was our opportunity.

After eating Dad's feast, Phil set off by himself on a private trek. He hiked up the draw's east-facing hill to the top of the ridge. He told me later that while gazing at the ranch house far below him and at the surrounding countryside, he had experienced a small epiphany. It started when his ears began ringing, which he figured was caused by the quiet. He heard only the sounds the birds and bugs made while going about their daily chores. With a surprising decision settling in his heart, he slipped and slid his way on loose soil back down the mountain, past ignimbrite boulders snuggled into the hillside and thickets of gnarly junipers until he reached the driveway. When Phil entered the bright-yellow ranch kitchen, he announced, like Moses after descending the mountain, that he was crazy about the place. He hadn't even thrown a hook in the river. The plump trout had yet to shudder at his name. In the blink of an eye, Dad's offer at breakfast became a reality.

His plan was to fix up the ranch hand's house at the base of Rosebud Draw. He wanted us to live there and watch the place while he was away on his numerous business trips. "You two can do your leatherwork in the garage-studio," he said, "and send it off to the galleries in Portland." So the deal was done.

Before we left to return to the city, Dad took us to the little house that would eventually become our home for the next twenty-five years. It was worse than a shack. It sat seventy feet off the county road. A raggedy fence surrounded a yard of dandelions, cheat grass, and patches of dirt. The old grey-ridged asphalt siding hung in disarray off the tiny house. Small, flyspecked windows stared back at us. We stepped onto the porch, careful not to put our sandals through the broken boards, and passed a partially hinged screen door. The dented and chipped front door opened into a huge kitchen, where a hole made by wood rats revealed at least nine layers of vinyl flooring. The droppings of rats and mice covered the shelves, cabinets, sink, and stove. The rest of the house included a small bedroom, a bathroom the size of a public restroom cubicle, a short hall, and a living room comparable in size to the kitchen. This home belonged to the rodents, but I didn't care. I was crazy about it.

Over the next eleven months, Dad kept his promise, remodeling the tiny house and making it livable. Grumpy Joe Parton, who had accompanied Dad during one of his escapes from the state hospital, happened to be a carpenter, and Dad put him to work along with my eighteen-year-old nephew, Wade.

Grumpy and Wade fashioned the ratty little nine hundred square-foot house into a lovely home, at least on the inside. And although they painted the new porch and steps, entry door and screen door all a shiny white to match the house's interior, the rest of the exterior included a dull asphalt siding with a rolled tar paper roof, and sagging windows. But it didn't faze me a bit. I still loved it.

And finally, in the summer of 1974, Phil and I packed up our city lives in Portland and followed our destiny back over the trail to settle in the house on Rosebud Creek.

Best Place

I lay in bed next to the window, grinning as four reedy, falsetto voices drifted into the bedroom. "If theyyyyy could see me nowwww," the boys sang, with lots of fervor and a little bit of rhythm. "Those little friends of miiiiine," happily mangling the words from *Sweet Charity*.

Next to me, Phil snuffled awake, not nearly as appreciative as I. "What the—?"

"It's Wade, Rand, and the boys," I said, leaning over him. "They're serenading us." I threw off the light summer blanket and hurried to the window. A teenage, ragtag quartet—my nephews Wade and Rand, along with Ray and Tom—clad in T-shirts and jeans, all with long hair hanging past their shoulders, smiled back. They were plumb tickled with themselves. Our two huskies, Belle and Whitewater, sat in the grass next to them. I'd heard a howl or two from them. Any howling, or any sound resembling howling, and the huskies participated. We had many companionable howling sessions together.

"We wanted to sing you a welcome song for your first morning in Izee," Wade said. "Whatcha think?"

"It was perfect," I told them. I looked up at the deep, clear blue sky and wondered if it had *always* been so blue.

"Off-key," Phil added with a drowsy mumble, as he stepped beside me.

All four boys beamed. They had arrived from Las Vegas a few months earlier to help Dad work the ranch. Wade told us later—much later, after he was safely away from Nevada—that the four of them *had* to get away, had "stepped on some toes" during an unnamed, nefarious business deal. But on the ranch they worked hard and looked out for one another, and after adjusting to Izee's rural lifestyle, they began to thrive.

"Why are you guys here so early?" Phil asked, stifling a yawn. We'd tumbled into bed late after a grueling move of two hundred and fifty miles in a heavily-loaded 1970 Volkswagen bus. Wade and Ray had followed, driving a rented van loaded with a freezer, a tattered couch, our studio work benches, various mismatched chairs, and an oak bed and dresser we'd picked up at a transient motel on Front Street in Portland. The rest of the load consisted of large boxes filled with studio tools, kitchen utensils, and books.

Normally, we slept until nine or ten because we were city folk born and bred, and usually worked in the studio until two in the morning. Something, however, was different here. For the first time since childhood, I felt I should have been up for hours.

"We came to help unload your gear," said Tom, who resembled a young, friendly Karl Malden. He was eager to please and had a sweet, uncomplicated temperament. "Where do you want us to start?"

"Yeah," Ray chimed in. "Let's roll."

"I'll put on some coffee," I told them. The boys unloaded both rigs before the coffee stopped perking and put everything in the yard. With the dogs snuffing at our feet we had started going through it when Rand said, "Hey, look—it's Lennie Lipp!" A short man dressed all in brown marched into the driveway and up to the boys, who stood by the van with packing boxes tipped precariously in their arms.

Close-up, the man's skin had the same brown hue as his clothes, all the color coming from dirt. His face held an intense expression as if something important was on his mind. Resting across his arm was an old muzzleloading rifle. He was bowlegged and seemed plucky. I half-expected him to sing, "I yam what I yam and that's all what I yam. I'm Popeye the Sailor Man!"

"Lennie!" Rand said. "How are you today?"

"Good. Good," Lennie said. "Saw a coyote on the way here, out mebbe two hunnert yards and ah shot thet there coyote. Yep." He jutted his jaw pugnaciously and stared at the boys. Phil and I were near the front door, poring over a box of garden tools.

Wade looked over at us. "C'mere, Lennie," he said, "and meet our aunt and uncle."

Following Wade through the mounds of boxes, Lennie picked his way daintily, mindful not to bump anything.

"Lennie Lipp," Wade said, "meet Phil and Kristy"

Lennie quickly spat into his hands, ran them through his long, straight hair, and rubbed them on his filthy pants. Then he held out a hand for a shake.

Phil, brought up in a home that taught good manners, didn't hesitate. "My pleasure, Mr. Lipp."

"Yep, mine, too," Lennie said, giving Phil a handshake so vigorous that Lennie's hair once again fell to his eyes. He hawked another gob of spit into his palms, rubbed them together quickly, and combed his hair back. Then he turned to me.

Now, I wasn't a beauty, but I was young and had blonde hair down to my waist, an attribute that seemed to attract children as well as the armpits of strangers on windy days. I figured the hair must evoke the fairy princess thing. Lennie stared at it. A wondrous grin spread across his face. His left front tooth, roughly the width of our dining room table, appeared stubbornly perpendicular from its buddies and reached to within inches of my face.

"Ma'am," he said. "Whut do yew use on yore hahr? Yew know, ah use horse shampoo. It surely brings out the luster o' mine, doncha think?"

Hypnotized by the talking tooth, I still yammered something out. "Er...hair... ah...yes...so nice tooth—TO—meet you...I'm delighted, I'm sure."

I shot a look at the boys, expecting them to be watching my reaction. Oddly, they weren't paying us any mind. Tom found a speck of something on his shirt and was plucking madly at it. Ray instigated an impromptu wrestling session with Whitewater and Belle. Rand rubbed nonchalantly on a spot on the dirty van. Wade picked up four boxes meant for the studio and hurried into the house.

Phil finally jabbed me in the ribs to bring me to my senses. My mama didn't raise a cretin, either, so I said, "I think it's time for lunch! Lennie, would you like to join us? We're having peanut butter and jelly sandwiches."

Quickly, all the boys showed up directly behind Lennie, gesturing cut-off signs, pointing at their mouths, and shaking their heads. What's got into them? I thought.

I headed for the kitchen, the second biggest room in the house, and started whipping out sandwiches. Wade started to follow, but Lennie beat him to it, so Wade made a quick U-turn back outside again. In the close proximity of the house, the kitchen filled up quickly with an indescribable odor. It grew stronger as Lennie got closer to me.

"Got any Coca Cola?" It was a question he was to repeat every time I saw him over the next two years.

"Sorry, Lennie," I said. "We just don't drink it." A combination of disbelief and disappointment showed on his face. Later I learned that Coke was his nectar, and he was rarely without it. Well, maybe it will eventually rot his tooth, I reasoned.

When Lennie offered to help take out the food, I couldn't refuse without hurting his feelings, so I guiltily wrapped it with plastic so his personal debris didn't fall onto the sandwiches.

The guys all fell to eating as though the sandwiches were filet mignon, but I noticed they sat far away from Lennie. Within a minute of Lennie plopping down next to me, I knew the reason: He ate with his mouth wide open, and parts of his sandwich ended up on the platform tooth. In addition, his lively conversation included occasional outbursts of laughter that sent me dodging bits of sandwich. The trouble was that almost everything tickled him. He was a sweet person with a happy disposition, but I learned not to tell a joke during a meal with him.

After lunch, Rand gave Lennie a ride back to the Sloan ranch, where he worked. As soon as Lennie was gone, Wade told the story of the unfortunate fellow. It seemed that Bob Sloan found Lennie hanging around the gate at a cattle auction. After a few inquiries, Bob discovered that Lennie was homeless, so Bob hired Lennie as a "gateman" to open and close the gates for Bob's elderly father because it was too hard for the old man to climb in and out of the pickup as he made his rounds of the ranch.

In spite of Lennie's personal habits, the boys were kind to him. As he walked the twenty-mile radius that encompassed the eight ranches in the Izee area, they'd pick him up and take him where he wanted to go. If they saw a coyote, though, Lennie would make them stop so he could take a shot with his muzzleloader. After each shot he'd say, "I killed that coyote!" Ninety percent of the time, though, the bullet struck the ground far from the target. One day Wade challenged Lennie about this.

"Lennie got all riled up," Wade said, "and turned red and started yelling at me."

"I...did...so...hit...that...coyote!" Lennie told him. "You call me a liar?"

"God, it took me forever to quiet him down," Wade said. "It just wasn't worth it. The poor guy almost choked on his own spit he was so upset."

So here it was my first day in Izee, and I had met Lennie. I wondered what our other neighbors were like. But one thing seemed certain: For a man like Lennie, and maybe for all of us as well, this was probably the best place to be.

Cattle Drive

Gathered in the kitchen, munching warm oatmeal cookies, Wade, Phil, and I stared down at a Malheur National Forest map spread out on the table.

"Your dad's a month late getting his cows up there," Wade said, pointing to a spot on the map that represented two thousand acres of grass, "and if we don't move them there by tomorrow, he could lose his grazing permit." The problem was that only my dad knew the route to the allotment, and he had left again on another of his mysterious trips.

"We have to take a hundred Herefords to Morgan Creek," Wade said, looking up from the map. "And we could use help moving them."

Phil and I glanced at each other and raised our eyebrows in a silent question. Our first cattle drive. After a week in Izee, we hadn't thought we'd ever do *real* ranch stuff. After all, we worked with leather, not with the raw product; we made designs on their skin *after* they were dead. But the boys needed our help.

"Sure!" Phil said. "How hard can it be?" I nodded my agreement, smiling big.

In our brightly lit kitchen with our bellies full of fresh-baked cookies, it was easy to believe the cattle drive would be a walk in the park. Heck, we'd just be trailing behind cows with their sweet faces, brown eyes, and innovative hairdos.

We watched as Wade's finger traced the course on the map. It didn't seem far. "I think this is the way," he assured us. "We take 'em up Poison Creek, through the forest, up this draw, and over the hill. Seems simple."

The rest of us muttered various encouraging grunts. Satisfied, he continued. "We have only two horses, so Rand and Andy will ride the flanks of the herd to keep strays from wandering off. Phil, do you and Kristy want to follow in the pickup while Tom walks behind and pushes 'em?"

I shook my head. "Not me," I said. "I want to go on foot."

Wade straightened and shoved his hair back. "Then we'll meet at eight in the morning."

At 6 a.m. I woke up sweaty, a sign the day would be sweltering. I wanted to wear cut-offs, but the boys, who had been in Izee only months but already knew the local wisdom, said our legs would be scraped raw by the stiff, sharp grasses. "Long jeans are best," Tom said, "and we might run into snakes, so wear boots."

And so dressed in Levis and fitted western shirts—we'd bought them at a sale in Prineville in an effort to fit into our new lifestyle—we gobbled a breakfast of toast as I braided my hair, scattering crumbs among the strands, then wrapped a blue kerchief over my head for good measure. Phil tied his woven leather headband around his head to keep his hair out of his eyes, and we were off.

We drove the old ranch pickup to Poison Creek. The boys, bless their teenage hearts, had already brought the cows out of Rosebud Draw, moved them down the road, and pointed them up the creek in the right direction.

"We have to keep them moving," Wade said. "They'll want to graze along the way, and the heat will make them stop a lot. The calves will tire, and the cows will fight us because we're picking on their babies."

By the time I started walking behind the herd and Phil drove off in the pickup, it was ten o'clock. The air was still and sultry, the mid-July sun merciless. By mid-day the heat became almost unbearable. The only cowboy hat in evidence was Rand's. I caught glimpses of its straw whiteness bobbing up and down on the hillsides as he rode back and forth, fetching the strays. Ray's black hair was harder to spot because he was down in the bogs below the dirt road, riding alongside the creek.

Meanwhile, Wade, Tom, and I trudged close behind the herd, with Tom on the right and Wade in the middle while I took the left. At least, I think that's where the others were. The air was so thick with powdery grime I was sure I'd die of asphyxiation. Dust hid the calves and cows in front of us. The three of us didn't bother to visit because the cattle protested their move so noisily it drowned out any hope of conversation.

An hour later we hit a fringe of pines, which shaded us from the sun for a while. The cows slowed down, and their deafening racket diminished a few notches. I optimistically mirrored the herd's mood. This isn't too bad, I reasoned. It can't be too much farther. But then we reached the draw from hell.

My first clue that not all was rosy was when the herd began milling in a circle rather than continuing forward. Over the protesting cows came angry voices screeching and cussing, and Rand began making his way back to us, both his face and his horse, Danny, streaked with dark rivulets of dirt and sweat. Although I knew as much about horses as I did about quarks, I could tell Danny was played out. Phil got out of the pickup and joined us.

Rand stopped in front of us. I smelled damp horse. Danny's nostrils puffed in and out. "We take them up here and then onto the ridge," Rand said, pointing toward a slope hidden by billowing dust, "and then straight down into Soda Creek." Thankfully, the slope was invisible to me, or I might have chickened out.

"You're gonna have to start yelling loud and throwing sticks at the cows," Rand shouted over his shoulder as he turned Danny toward the mountain, "or they won't budge!" He began hollering at the herd as he worked his way among them. I watched until the dust swallowed both horse and rider.

Phil, Tom, Wade, and I spread out to push the animals upwards. We worked on instinct. If we crowded them enough, they'd get nervous and move forward. Miraculously, they started up the steep grade. Every once in a while I grabbed a stick or a pebble and threw it at a slow cow—making sure I didn't hit it— or muttered a low "Hah!" (Cussing, I thought, was for bad girls and loose women.)

Up the slope the vegetation grew dense with junipers, pines, and firs, and with thick-stemmed bushes of currents, sagebrush, rabbit brush, and snowberries; low growing bunchgrass, mule's ears, Indian paintbrush, and wild onions were thick underfoot, often tripping us if we didn't pay attention.

Centuries passed, or maybe an hour, and the torturous trek up that grade and behind those cattle gave me the first inkling that the fun was over. We would never reach the top, I thought. Because there *is* no top.

The three bulls in the herd, which weighed fifteen hundred pounds each, fell behind until they lumbered along directly in front of me. Desperate, I stepped boldly to their rears and swatted them sharply with a good-sized branch, not caring if they turned on me. If they tried, I'd chew their snouts right off their faces. My quiet "Hah's!" turned into blood-curdling, banshee-screeching threats complete with cussing more wicked than I could remember my dad ever using. But soon I noticed mine was the only human voice. I looked around. Rand and Ray sat motionless on their horses, staring at me; Phil, Wade, and Tom stood the same way—watching me.

"WHAT?" I said.

"YOU'RE CUSSING!" Phil shouted above the cows' clamor. He was grinning.

"SO—WHAT'S YOUR POINT?" I gave them my best glare of disgust and threw a branch with an enormous burl towards a Hereford bull. It nailed him on his haunch. He inched ahead slightly but then stopped again. Finally, the guys got over their amazement of my transformation from angel to girl-from-hell, and the two horsemen rode at the bull, pushing him to climb. He'd move a little at a time, his breath gasping and his mouth foaming.

At the top of the ridge, the bull made a last ditch effort to escape his tormentors and moved under a granddaddy juniper tree. No matter how hard the boys tried to move him, he just stood his ground and stared at them. Finally, he lay down and died. Feeling terrible, we gathered around the poor animal, staring down at him and trying to find a reason for his death.

"Maybe he was too hot."

"Did we push him too hard?"

"Was he old?"

"Dibs on the horns!"

This from Rand. Although it seemed callous, it woke us from our reverie. Reluctantly, we left the bull to the elements. The rest of the cows needed our attention.

Magically energized once they reached the peak of Airplane Ridge, the cows started down the other side where the cool waters of Soda Creek awaited them near the bottom. Here, exhausted and thirsty, we collapsed along the bank and sucked up the dirty water.

After snoozing on the grass for a half-hour, we started on the last leg of the journey, which began with a half-hour's climb up a shorter hill. Once the cows reached the top, they trotted down the long slope to Morgan Creek, where they spread out under the swaying pines. It was over.

As cattle drives go, it could have been worse. Thunder and lightning, flash floods and hail storms, stampeding cows and horse wrecks could have been on the menu, so we skirted some scary stuff. But it was bad enough. I was certain about one thing, though: Never again would I do a cattle drive on foot. Instead, I would learn to ride a horse. From now on, let the horse walk behind the cows.

Izee Deliverance

Knock-knock-knock. Someone was at my door, and I hadn't lived in Izee long enough to have visitors. Who was it? After all, it was *rural* out here on County Road 63. John Day, the nearest town of any size, was forty-two miles away. Ranches surrounded me, but the spread was wide. The nearest neighbor was a mile away, and somebody could rape and pillage me before anyone discovered my mutilated body. So in my first days on this solitary ranch, this city girl and horror film fan had come to assume that murderers, drug dealers, and demon worshippers who disembowel living things all passed by my house on a daily basis. So—*who was out there?*

With my front door situated all wrong to see the perpetrator, I did what I always told my friends and family *never* to do—I opened the door.

A tall, thin man with an unmistakably friendly face stood before me, holding his cowboy hat in his hands. Being an amateur student of body language, I recognized a respectful stance. A thankful sigh escaped my lips.

"May I help you?" I asked him, looking him over in spite of my reassurance. After his first rather surprised glance at me, he lowered his head, seemingly interested in the boards at my feet.

"Mizz Sinclar?" he mumbled into his collar.

"Yes?" I said, trying out my best responsible-grown-up voice. At twenty-four I still had a hard time thinking of myself as Mrs. Anything.

"Mizz Sinclar, ma'am. Ahm Charlie Wheatly from Malheur. Ah wuz up on yore forest permit an' cum acrost a bool with yore tag an' so ah put him in a crail already built up thur so's yew can git 'im." Once the man started up, he boiled over with words streaming out of him. They just kept coming. I was enraptured, spellbound.

"It's up whur the 6370 road meets the 373? Caps? Thet allotment? Raht close to a spring box. Yew probly know the spot. Ah know yer outta there an' the bool holed up when yew moved." He paused and waited, swaying from one foot to the other.

I guessed it was my turn and managed a "Oh, uh huh?"

"Ah spied sum kivs in the willers so's yew might give a look to thim. Couldn't see the muthurs. Left behind, too, mebbe." He went on for another five minutes, going into deep explanations. Each time it seemed appropriate, I nodded, grunted a reply, or smiled encouragingly. After he was finished, he bobbed his head and worried his hat.

"Wahl...'kay then. 'S bin a pleasure, ma'am." Then he was gone.

When Phil came home later, he asked me what kind of a day I'd had.

"Well, a man stopped, and I opened the door."

Phil let out an involuntary gasp, one hand grabbing the edge of the table, the other clutching his chest. "You *what*?"

We were both fear-mongers, trained well from all the movies we'd seen. In this case, I knew Phil was thinking of *Deliverance*, the 1970s movie in which three city guys go on a camping trip, and some backwoods weirdoes do unspeakable things to one of them and almost kill all of them. We were trying to fit into the Izee environment and wanted to be friendly, but we were still on guard and wary of the occasional mad strangler.

"Well, he was friendly but shy," I said. "It was the way he stood there, hat in hand. I promise next time to be more careful."

"Okay," Phil said, slightly mollified, maybe because he was relieved I'd survived. "What did he want?"

"I have no idea. Couldn't understand a word he said. He may have been speaking a foreign language."

By asking around, we eventually discovered that Charlie Wheatly was the U.S. Forest Service employee who managed my father's grazing permit on the Malheur National Forest. We also discreetly ferreted out the meaning of the few key words

I remembered. We discovered, for example, that "kivs" are "calves," "bools" are "bulls," "crail" is "corral," and "willers" are "willows." A piece of cake, once you get into the rhythm of it.

A few months later, more strangers arrived at our house. I heard them before I saw them—Harley's! Big, bad-ass Harley Davidsons. *Bikers*. Oh, good lord! And Phil was in the front yard! They'll tear him to shreds, I thought.

But why would they stop here? Because they think Phil is a redneck rancher and for a lark want to beat one up? They had no idea Phil hadn't had enough time to become a redneck rancher since we'd only been in Izee for a couple of months. In fact, he still looked something like a 1960s hippie. Oh—that was it! They wanted to beat up a hippie. Gawd!

Hunkering down, I duck-walked to the window to peek out. What to do, what to do? Slowly I peered over the sill. Phil had his back to me, talking to a huge biker covered with black leather from head to heels. His ripped sleeves revealed massive biceps, and he must have stood 6 foot-9, towering over Phil's measly (but very manly) 5-10.

I backed quickly away from the window. I couldn't lock the door because they were standing too close to it, and the villain might hear the click and go ballistic. Meanwhile, Phil was probably thinking, *I wish Kristy would bring out the twelve-gauge!*

On the other hand, I reasoned, maybe the guy was waiting for his chance to jump Phil and torture him, making him reveal the fact that a helpless woman was inside the house. I edged over to the window again, this time from a different vantage point in case the biker had already spotted me and was just acting cagey, like he hadn't seen me.

Now I saw *three more* bikers. This was too much. Phil didn't have a chance. After they murdered him, they'd undoubtedly storm the house and terrorize me into telling them where the guns were. Then would come the rape and pillage—unless I'm not their type, in which case they'd just torture and kill me for the guns. Believe me, I know how this kind of man thinks. And Phil knows I know and is waiting for me to act. Poor guy!

I slithered back down and scooted across the floor to the gun rack. But just as I reached for it, the door opened. Startled, I jerked wildly, caught my braid in a rifle's bolt, and pressed my face against the wall, panting like a trapped animal.

"Well, that was interesting." It was Phil. Speaking calmly.

"Wha—what happened out there?" I managed to croak.

Phil stepped over and untangled my hair from the rifle. "They need gas for their bikes," he said. "You know how the map shows Izee as a town, so they thought they could fill up here. I sent them down to Johnson's." He grabbed a warm cookie off the cookie sheet.

"No, no—that won't do! Phil, I saw the Johnson men go by this morning with their horse trailers. June is down there alone!" I ran to the phone to call her. It was dead. A typical occurrence because the lines were old. "You've got to go and warn her!"

"He seemed like a nice guy. He walked up to me and said, 'We're in kind of a pickle,' so I knew he was okay."

We're in kind of a pickle? What kind of biker quotes Shakespeare? Still, it could be a ploy. "We've got to see if she's okay. C'mon."

I grabbed a cookie and stuffed it in his mouth before he could start grumbling—he *loved* praline cookies—then seized his hand, shot out the door, and headed for the car.

"Let's drive up slowly in case we have to get the jump on them," I suggested as we turned into the Johnson's driveway.

"Why are you whispering?" he asked.

I gave him a look that said *How can you ask that*, even though we were the only ones in the car and the rapist and pillagers were still a half-mile away.

When we reached the house, we didn't see anyone. It was downright deserted. Very ominous. A bad sign, indeed.

"They've already got her," I whispered.

Phil parked the car and got out. "June," he called. "Are you here?" I could tell he was getting antsy. About time.

"Hello-o-o," answered a sweet voice. "I'm in the back by the garden."

My gosh, the relief! We rounded the house to the garden.

"Did the bikers stop here?" Phil asked her.

I was looking around, on alert, in case it was a trap. I watched her closely for any signs of trauma.

"Oh, yes. Lovely people. They parked on the road and sent their ladies to ask if they could buy some gas. I guess they thought I might be spooked if the men came. I don't know what made them think that. We're friendly people out here."

Obviously, June is a nice person but extremely naive about serial killers on the prowl. I vowed that very soon I would explain to her how things work in the *real* world. Or, at least, in *my* world.

Buckaroo Wisdom

When our life in Izee began, Phil and I thought we would work in our studio on the ranch and maybe help out with the chores once in awhile. But that was before we discovered that here—smack dab in the middle of eastern Oregon's cowboy country—the ranch work never ended.

Our first fall season on the ranch, for example, we needed to gather the cows for auction. But because Dad had left on a hasty business trip to San Francisco before contacting the auction yard, the job was left to Phil and Wade, who knew that two inexperienced horsemen weren't enough to ride six thousand acres of slate hillsides covered with ropey sagebrush and prickly junipers. So Phil called the auction yard in Vale and explained the situation.

"Not to worry Mr. St. Clair," said Red MacDuff, owner of the auction yard. "My two top buckaroos and I are chomping at the bit for some action and would purely love a couple days of a good gather."

"That's great." Phil told him. "The old ranch house up Poison Creek has beds, food, and running water."

"Then we'll see you Friday at daybreak."

Friday morning as the sun peeked over Mt. Mahogany, Phil and Wade saddled up, and the outfit from the auction yard drove in. Accompanying Mr. MacDuff—a dapper, friendly man—were his two cowboys, Mushy and Junior. Mushy, who resembled the cook Wishbone from the 1950s television western *Rawhide*, looked like he'd seen a few round-ups. His face was covered with thick, wiry hair that turned out to be made up of eyebrows, nose hairs, and a moustache. During the introductions, the top half of this bush wiggled madly up and down while one eye would suddenly appear on one side or the other, but both eyes never showed at the same time.

Junior, a young and very shy boy, wore the biggest cowboy hat ever seen this side of a sombrero. The crown stood up a foot high, and the brim shaded most of the boy's shoulders.

"The day is yet a pup, boys," Mr. MacDuff said after the hand shaking was over. "Let's get at her."

They brought out two Appaloosas and a black Quarter horse, all beauties. Stumpy and Goofy, other horses from Dad's "string," watched forlornly over the fence. Wade noticed Junior eyeing them. "Paul says no one rides these two much," Wade told him. "Goofy's green-broke and Stumpy bucks."

"*Ah'll* ride Stumpy fur yew," Junior said softly.

"Junior weel tek the buck outta thet horse," Mushy said, assuring everyone. It seemed like a good idea that someone wanted to work Stumpy, so Junior turned his Appy out to the horse pasture, saddled Stumpy, and they all rode out.

The gather started at Soda Creek. Wade and Junior disappeared up into the draws and ridges while Phil, Mushy, and Red worked the sides and meadow. By noon, the three bottom riders were trailing close behind some fast-moving, squirrelly yearlings. At the gate, the young cattle spooked and turned into the Soda Swamp. Red and Mushy plowed on through the muck. Phil was following when his horse, Dan, mired down.

The horse lunged, looking for footing. Phil hopped off and held the reins until Dan found solid ground. Mushy and Red couldn't stop to help. They turned the cows and headed them out the gate and onto the highway. Phil finally caught up, riding next to Mushy.

Mushy was antsy. It was clear he had something to say. The old cowboy's shaggy eyebrows were jumping around like small critters. "Now Pheeul," he said, gnawing on his chew then shooting an impressive stream between his teeth. "Yew kin tek this or yew kin walk away from it but don't *never* git off'n yore horse in a bog hole!"

"But," Phil said, "I—"

"Yew see," continued the cowboy, "a horse is jest lookin' anywhere to move outta his predikyment and it jest might be climbin' over yore body next time." Mushy scrutinized Phil a few heartbeats to see if he understood.

"Oh, okay," Phil said. "Thanks, Mushy." Phil was grateful; he'd just learned a valuable lesson he could store away for future reference.

"Mah pleasure, ah'm sure."

While Phil, Red, and Mushy moved their cows up the highway, Wade and Junior took different routes to flush out other cows from the draws and ridges. Wade took the low side of Soda Creek, and Junior traveled along the rims. Between Elk Horn and Soda, Wade picked up a lone cow and calf. As he pushed them down the ravine, he heard a ruckus above him.

"IS THAT ALL YEW CAN GIVE ME, SON? WHAT ARE YEW, A RED HEADED STEP CHILE? HA, HA, HA!"

Wade looked up. It was Junior. Stumpy was arched in mid-air with Junior's skinny body snapping crazily above the wild gelding. Junior's big hat was still intact.

"C'MON, BOY! HA, HA, HEE, HEE, HEE! TAKE IT OUTTA LOW AND SHOVE IT ON IN TO HIGH GEAR! YEEEEHAH! ALL RIGHT! NOW YUR TAWKIN', POTLIKKER! YAHHOOOEEE!"

In a whirl of dust, horse and rider disappeared over the hill. Trampled, uprooted sagebrush and overturned rocks tumbled down in their wake. Spooked by the rodeo, the cow and calf took off, so Wade had no choice but to follow without knowing the outcome of Junior's and Stumpy's communication problem.

Later, when Wade arrived back at the corrals, Junior and a subdued Stumpy trailed in, pushing four pairs. Junior rode slightly higher in the saddle. Wade asked the cowboy how things had gone, halfway expecting a colorful explanation of victory. Instead, his voice barely above a whisper and with a flicker of a smile, Junior murmured, "Oh, fair to middlin', ah reckon."

The next morning, with the previous day's gather of cows in the holding pasture, Wade was left to catch up on chores while the others met at the bottom of Poison Creek. The rest of the cattle were scattered two miles up on the steep hillsides. The plan was to ride up to the head of the draw, and from there push the cattle back down to the road. The buckaroos seemed extra cheerful, maybe at the prospect of a good job near its finish.

"Ya know, ah've got the fastest horse heer," Mushy said. "Nothin' kin beat 'im."

"Ah don' think so, Mush," Junior mumbled, either forgetful of the condition that had him riding high in the saddle or just too young to pay it any mind. "This heer Appy looks mighty fit to mah eyes."

"Not as fit as mah Tequila, ah'll wager," Mush said, his eyebrows growing agitated.

"Is that a challenge I'm hearing, boys?" Red was astride his magnificent black Quarter horse.

"Mebbe," Mushy said. "Mebbe not. And mebbe ah'll jest show yew. Meetcha at the ranch house! HAH!" He spurred his horse and shot off.

Red and Junior gave chase, slapping leather for all they were worth. Phil, half-asleep on Dan, was thinking, I don't have any dogs in this fight, when Dan suddenly exploded beneath him. Phil's boots scrabbled for stirrups and one hand clawed desperately for the saddle horn as Dan easily blazed past the others. Much later, as the men pulled up in the ranch yard, Phil was waiting for them, trying out a look of nonchalance.

"Well, crap on a stick," Mushy said as he came in dead last, his hat askew and kept on only by the tentacles of his untamed hair. "Wah didn't yew say yore horse could run?"

"It ain't even fair to jest lead a man on lek thet," breathed Junior.

"Not sporting, Mr. St. Clair," added MacDuff. "No, not at all."

After the Poison Creek gather, the good nature of the cowboys made them quickly forget their loss, and the last of the cows were brought to the corrals. While driving the stragglers up the county highway, Phil thought it was a good time to give our young dog Rooster some practice working cows. But Rooster continually ended up in the wrong spot, either getting in front of the cattle and stopping them, or coming between a mother and her calf. The worse Rooster got, the more Phil hollered at him.

Mushy, riding close to Phil and mining dirt out from under his fingernails with the same knife he'd used to carve his apple at lunch, sadly shook his wooly head, throwing billows of trail dirt into the air. "Pheeul," he said, an expression of benevolent patience settling on his face. "Do…not…be…yellin'…at…yore…dawg. Jest let 'im chew a leetle."

"Really?" Phil said. "Well, I think he'll just—"

"Nosir. Ah'm tellin' yew. Throw rocks at 'im, stomp on 'im, or beat on 'im but don' never *yell* at yore dawg."

Later at the corral Rooster, happily undisciplined, for the third time stopped a bunch of cows from being funneled into the gate.

"DAMMIT NOW, DAWG!" Mushy screeched, his face contorted and red, his hands clenched at his side. "ENUF IS ENUF!" He gave Phil a severe look. "What is *wrong* with yore *dawg!* Yew need to keep 'im outta thet crail! Yew jest can't let 'im run loose like thet! Good *Gawd,* man!"

The last cattle truck was ready to go as the day closed in on sundown. The work was almost finished when the last calf escaped from the corral into the horse pasture. The men herded it back to the corral, but Goofy, who seemed lonesome for some company, came in, too, and the confused calf hunkered under him.

"Rope that horse, boys," Red told them matter-of-factly.

Junior and Mushy started swinging their lassoes, each throwing a loop. Goofy stood perfectly still as Mushy's rope landed on his nose.

"Lord, look at 'im duck thet loop," Mushy shouted. His next throw lit on Goofy's motionless haunch and rolled off. The old horse yawned.

"Thet horse bin roped afore," Junior announced, his loop hitting at least a foot in front of Goofy. The horse's eyes started to close with boredom.

After a few more throws never came close to Goofy, Mushy turned to his boss. "Mr. MacDuff," he said, "thet horse is plumb unropeable." The three men nodded in solemn agreement. Goofy turned, scaring the calf out from under him, and sauntered out the open gate and back into the horse pasture. The calf was then hustled into the truck with little fanfare.

So with goodbye handshakes and some affable joshing, the buckaroos loaded their horses and left, driving east and following the last truck. As they headed up the old asphalt highway, it's likely their conversation turned to how they were able to help out the greenhorns of Izee and impart their buckaroo wisdom where it was needed. Or maybe each man pondered his part of the visit. Something along the lines of, "A tidy sum of money," or "Ah niver yet met the horse thet could buck me off," or "Mebbe ah should git ma hahr trimmed jest a mite."

Small Critters

The harsh environment of the high desert seems to encourage breeding of the creepiest life forms. Bugs, rodents, and snakes *love* it here. Armies of furry or scaly or hard-shelled little creatures *thrive*. In eastern Oregon, however, folks live in a benign co-existence with these creatures, the ranchers accepting them all as part of rural living. Nevertheless, we still thought like west-siders, where mice and rats aren't allowed in the house, and where snakes are easygoing and beneficial. As a result, we mistakenly believed we presided over our new domain. But it took only a few confrontations before it sunk in that the small critters rule here.

Our first lesson arose in the dim light of sunset on our first summer's night in Izee. With our household stuff still packed in boxes, the four boys living in the ranch house then—Wade, Rand, Ray, and Tom—invited us to dinner. As we strolled in to their driveway in our sandals (we were soon to discover why no one wore open-toed shoes on a ranch), the boys stood waiting for us, smiling.

"We want to show you something," Rand said, all excited. "We nabbed it in the bar pit. We call him King." The boys stepped aside, revealing a ramshackle cage fashioned from rotted fence posts topped with rusty window screen. We approached, thinking they'd captured a baby porcupine or badger. All of us stood gazing down into its murky interior.

The boys abruptly stopped chattering and looked at one another "Where is he?" said Ray. "Did somebody let him go?"

"Oh no." whispered Tom. "Look." He pointed to the corner where the wire was pushed up.

"Let what go?" Phil asked. "It can't be that bad."

None of the boys answered. They stared at our sandals. As if reading one another's minds, they began easing their way towards the kitchen door.

"King's the biggest rattlesnake we've ever seen," Wade called back over his shoulder. "He must be old, too, because his rattles are gone."

Great. A silent rattler. No warning before two venomous fangs began pumping poison into tender flesh. Phil and I bolted for the door, passing the boys along the way.

They never found King.

This episode became the foundation for the involuntary blind panic that set in later with the appearance of a snake. Any snake. Our body's fight or flight mechanism always took over, and we couldn't be responsible for our actions.

A week after King's disappearance, for example, we decided our yard needed attention. While we concentrated on taming clumps of nettles and knee-high Kentucky bluegrass, our two huskies, Belle and Whitewater, started barking feverishly at something they'd cornered. Phil investigated and found a coiled rattler. The only sound he could utter was "URGHEEE!"

After a couple more gurgling noises, he was able to make words: "KRISTY!" he screeched, "CALL THE DOGS AND HOLD ONTO THEM IT'S A SNAKE I'M GONNA GET SOMETHING TO KILL IT!" He disappeared into the shed.

The dogs and I waited. Phil was gone so long that the snake had enough time to find a mate and make more snakes.

"OKAY," Phil said, returning at last. "THESE SHOULD DO IT." Crisscrossed in his arms like oversized pick-up sticks were all our yard tools.

"Are you going to drop all those on the snake?" I asked.

He gave me a you're-being-sarcastic look but calmed down. "Noooo. Try to be serious, Kristy. I brought them all so I could determine the best tool for the job, and this," he said, holding up a shovel, "is perfect."

Then, after relocating the snake, he whacked it with the shovel approximately twenty times more than necessary. "I'd like to save the skin to tan," he said, holding up the mangled carcass. "Next time I'll smash the head and save the body."

The opportunity to do that arose later in the summer. We were kneeling on ancient, grayed barn boards, using pry bars to pull out six-inch nails, when Phil heard a muffled buzzing. He hopped off the board and turned it over. A small rattlesnake lay coiled between two planks.

"GULGEREEBLE!" he said.

I instantly translated Phil's new-found language into "Oh, geez—a snake!"

"FOR GOD'S SAKE STAY BACK!" he yelled. At the time I sat a good twelve feet away, next to a toppled barn wall. "I'LL GET HIM WITH THIS PRY BAR."

"Phil, remember you were going to save the—"

BAM-BAM-BAMMITY-BAM-BAM-BAM-BAM! The tiny snake was an unrecognizable mashed stain on the board.

"My gosh! I don't know what came over me!" Phil said, shaking his head. "It's just that the creepy things are everywhere, and they take you by surprise!"

But some of those surprises happened *inside* the house and didn't involve snakes at all. For example, one night as we lay reading in bed, a strange noise came from the corner.

Scritchity.

"Phil?" I said, *The Hobbit* hardback perched on my stomach. "Did you hear that?"

Phil, already deep into *The Fellowship of the Rings*, was not eager to converse. "What?" he said, yawning.

Scritchity. Scritchity.

"That!" I told him. "Something's in here besides us."

"I hear nothing." This is the norm. I sleep lightly, have great hearing, and can detect any odor. It's surprising the CIA and FBI haven't visited our home as recruiters. Conversely, Phil slumbers like the dead, and wouldn't notice if the milk had soured. To be fair, I can't spot a deer a mile away on a bushy hillside like he can. In the fog. At dusk.

Scritchity. Scritchity. Scritchity.

"Did you guys hear that?" Wade bounded into our bedroom from his couch-bed in the living room.

Scritchity.

"In there!" Wade pointed at the closet. Phil leaped out of bed, tumbling Tolkien off his chest. The two started throwing out shoes, boxes, and hats, searching for the intruder. When one shoebox remained, they hand-signaled their next move. Phil seized the last box and lifted it. Huddled in the corner was a tiny field mouse.

"Ah-HAH!" They yelled, and quickly bent closer to get a better look.

Meanwhile, the mouse, suddenly galvanized to action, charged straight upward at their faces, which immediately registered disbelief and terror.

"AIIIIIEEEEEHHHHHHHH!" Phil dropped the box; they lurched backwards, spun around, and vaulted onto the bed.

"Why didn't you thump it?" Wade asked Phil. "You had it dead to rights!"

"Me! What about you? You're supposed to be the tough I-was-in-a-Vegas-gang kid!"

"It's not a normal mouse!"

"Well, we'll get it this time."

Wade looked aghast at Phil. "Not me."

They had a brief stare down. Phil sighed. Gathering his dignity, he cautiously slid off the bed, slowly grabbed a shirt, and in a flash hurled it over the area where the mouse cowered. Then Phil pounced on the shirt and trapped the mouse. After my pleas to let the plucky little guy live, Phil put him out into the night. The next day every possible entry way in the house had a tin can lid nailed over it. After that, unless someone left the door open, all the mice stayed out.

Not long after, another encounter with an even smaller critter happened when Dad invited Phil's folks to stay at the ranch house for a weekend while he went to Reno on business. The four of us spent the day strolling along the riverbank, watching the trout and shiners seize the wiggling grasshoppers we threw to them. After a dinner of grilled hamburgers, Mom and Pop went back to the ranch house to bed. Early the next morning the phone rang. Phil answered it.

"Hi, Mom. Dad has a *what*?" He started to chuckle. "Where? Oooohhhh, noooo. Hahahaha." Suddenly he stopped laughing. "But, Mom—you can get it as easily as I can." Chatter spilled out of the phone. "Please try again, okay?"

Phil looked uncomfortable. "I'd...rather...not, Mom. Uh huh. Oh, all right. I'll be right up." He turned to me. "A tick found a home underneath Pop's testicles," he said. "Mom can't get to it, so she wants me to try. Pop doesn't think it's so funny."

A half hour later, Phil was back. "First Mom poured us each a shot of whiskey," he explained. "Then Dad dropped his pants. Mom handed me the tweezers. Pop, sort of, you know, lifted them up for me. 'Careful, son,' he told me. And at that moment, the three of us lost it. We laughed so hard, tears streamed down our faces. Mom gave me a couple more shots to steady my hand, and I plucked it off. Isn't there any place these small critters won't invade?"

Probably not. Eastern Oregon seems to belong to small critters. And nothing is off limits to them. Not even a man's privates.

First Christmas

A week before our first Izee Christmas, three things happened in succession: It started snowing, we attended the Izee School Christmas party, and our relatives arrived for the holidays. That last event caused fear and trembling. Our families were as different from each other as William Shakespeare (St. Clairs) was from Danielle Steele (Timm). Would they get along? Add into the brew the fact that Phil's family disapproved of our move to eastern Oregon.

But first came the snow. And as it collected cheerfully in our high desert valley, who could worry about relatives? Our straggly yard with its broken wire fence turned into an enchanting sculpture. Phil shoveled meandering corridors. Belle and Whitewater, our Siberian huskies, leaped in the snow like whitetail deer. With their noses plowing through the icy fluff and their heads lifting to make sure we watched them, they flashed us tongue-lolling dog grins. What a joy to live where it looked and felt like Christmas.

Then came the party. The yuletide spirit ran high throughout our little community, and soon a neighbor called. Or, rather, several neighbors. At the same time.

"Kristy?" Gwen Sheehan's friendly voice echoed over our party line. "Has anyone invited you two to the school party?"

"KRISTY…ST.…CLAIR," boomed Angus Sheehan, Gwen's father-in-law, inviting himself into the conversation from his own phone. "SANTA WILL BE THERE."

"Hi Angus," I said. "Uh...Gwen?"

"You really shouldn't miss the kid's party, hon," interrupted another woman. It sounded like Lana from up the highway. "Being new people an' all."

Gwen broke in. "It starts at—"

"THEY'll HAVE CANDY."

"For the *children,* Angus," snorted Lana. "And by the way, Santa shouldn't bring a whiskey flask to a school party." Angus took offense and the rubberneckers began bickering.

"Kristy, it's at six o'clock on December 19," Gwen finished quickly. "You'll meet more neighbors! Bye!"

Before I hung up, the last snatch of conversation I heard involved Lana and Angus debating who had trespassed over a fenceline in 1959.

The night of the school gathering, the fresh snow promised to make it festive. The old schoolhouse sat high off the ground on a rock foundation. As Phil and I climbed the disjointed stairs and stepped into the crowded room warmed by a rumbling oil heater, we saw familiar neighbors and noticed a few strangers giving us curious glances. Eventually they drifted over and introduced themselves. Off to the side, Lennie waved wildly at us while sitting near his elderly boss, Will Sloan. Lennie had spiffed up for the party, slicking his hair back into a dashing ducktail. We scooted onto the bench next to the Sheehans and waited for the program.

Four kids—three boys and one girl, ages ten to thirteen—ambled out from behind the piano. Each recited original poems and then bellowed "Deck the Halls" with holiday gusto. As it ended, their parents led a thunderous applause. Then the teacher pounded away on the upright piano, encouraging us to sing along on "Oh Come, All Ye Faithful." Baritones, altos, and sopranos warbled unidentifiable notes that somehow merged in neighborly goodwill. Soon after, Gwen and a young woman with waist-length blonde hair brought out the refreshments. She was Amy, Jeff Gallagher's fiancé. She and gentle Gwen would become my lifelong friends.

Phil and I mixed with fellow partygoers while balancing paper plates full of taffy, fudge, and candy canes. Mounds of tinted sugar-sprinkled cookies, holiday stollen, savory dips, store-bought crackers, and sliced venison sausages dotted the papered tables. In the corner, a small cluster of smiling men drew flasks from beneath heavy jackets and then dribbled the contents into their punch.

A boy sidled up and offered me a tiny meatball on a toothpick. "Please try one," he said. "You'll love it." His twin sat nearby, snickering and watching intently. My brain's radar zinged a warning, but I'd seen a woman eat one earlier, and she was still alive. So I took one.

"Thanks," I told him. "Ummm. It tastes like a hot dog."

The two boys began laughing hard. "They're calf balls!" they shouted. "Hahahaha. She ate testicles!"

The door suddenly banged open, and there stood a very short and rosy-skinned Santa. "HO-HO-HO!" burst forth from his crooked white beard. He waddled past me, winked, and whispered, "It's me. *Angus.*"

Kids and adults swarmed around him. From his enormous velvet sack he pulled out small bags filled with oranges, nuts, and hard candies that he handed out to everybody, and then he shot back out the door yelling, "MERRY CHRISTMAS!" as it banged shut behind him.

Santa's appearance ended the party. It was 7:30 and people yawned, said it was their bedtime, and drifted out to their trucks. Old friends yelled to one another.

"Merry Christmas, ya old outlaw."

"You, too. Come by for a drink o' whiskey if you're able, and play pinochle."

Warmth rushed through me, filling me with gratitude for being in Izee. These people enjoyed one another. Loved one another's kids. Welcomed strangers. Maybe I *was* ready for our families to visit. I'd find out in two days.

To prepare for that visit, the next day Wade, Phil, and I went looking for a Christmas tree. We drove up Poison Creek, where the pines and firs bunched together, but most were trees only Dr. Seuss could love. We trudged up the hill through two feet of crusty snow, and while Phil and Wade chopped down a bushy Douglas fir, I gathered greenery for boughs.

That night while looking for decorations upstairs at Dad's house, I found a beat up box left behind by Don Jones, the previous ranch owner. Some tattered ornaments, a faded crocheted snowman, a torn school photo of a smiling child, a broken glass cherub—these represented a family who had once celebrated Christmas together here. I hung the ornaments on Dad's tree. If nothing else, it reminded me to be grateful for the love of family and friends—a good thing to remember during the relatives' Christmas visit.

The next day they arrived. Dad had flown into Portland and then hitched a ride to Izee with Phil's parents, while Mom drove from Bend, 120 miles away.

"Our families," Phil told me, "could test even Santa's good nature." He sat on a stool, milking the two front teats of Angie, our milk cow. On Angie's other side I sat, squeezing her two smaller teats as we squirted milk into the same bucket.

That night at Dad's house, butter from Angie's rich cream made herbed dips that were part of our Christmas Eve Smorgasbord—lefse, lutefisk, ham, scalloped potatoes, and raw vegetables. It was a Vikings' feast, though Wade said it was food that only a pregnant woman would eat.

Afterwards, we sat in the living room around Dad's tree, presents stacked high underneath. So far, the cheerful mood prevailed, though I still had a sense of dread in knowing that Phil's parents thought we had made a huge mistake in moving here. I wondered what kind of problems that disapproval was sure to cause.

"Get that big red box out first," Pop suggested, "the one that says 'From Mom and Pop to Phil.'"

Slowly Phil unwrapped his present. Inside lay a tan Stetson cowboy hat. Phil stuck it tentatively on his head. It sat crooked. But when he straightened it, he seemed transformed, as though he had taken another step closer to becoming a rancher.

His dad smiled at him. "We decided if you're gonna live out here, you have to have a proper hat," he said. "Merry Christmas, son."

Hard Winter

It was winter and we were alone. But we were too ignorant to realize exactly what that meant. After Dad and the boys had high-tailed it to warmer pastures, a neighbor's ominous warning began echoing in my ears as I watched Phil maneuver the Homelite chain saw in and out of the fallen tree he was cutting into firewood. "Eastern Oregon winters can be *brutal*," she had said with feeling. "So you'd best *prepare* before it strikes."

Both of us wrote her off as a histrionic woman trying to get a scare out of us. What could be difficult about winter? After all, we were young and strong. Besides, Portland rarely had snow, and I looked forward to having two or three feet of it. So without a care in the world, Phil finished cutting the last of the winter fuel for our little cast iron woodstove, and we felt sure we were ready. Bring it on, I thought. Unfortunately, that's exactly what happened.

Soon after placing the last split log onto our wood pile, the first wave of unrelenting cold started creeping into the Izee Valley. The sky took on a steely look, and the air grew as quiet as a church on Monday morning. When the smoke from our fire rose straight from the stovepipe—we didn't know this heralded a frigid shift in atmospheric conditions—the birds stopped singing, and the bugs began hiding in the nooks and crannies of our house.

Then Phil figured out something was up when he stuck his head outside and his nose hairs instantly froze. "Oh my gosh," he said. "Kristy, c'mere and look at this!"

In my nightie and slippers I followed Phil out onto the crackly grass of our yard. What a sight! The top half of a white-faced moon balanced on the eastern hills, illuminating the whole valley like a partially processed photograph. It was thrilling.

"The air is so still," he whispered, "that I can hear dogs barking at the ranch almost a mile away."

But it was also so cold that we soon rushed back into our heated kitchen. Before going to bed, we carefully banked the heavy logs in the wood stove, but in the morning they were reduced to lumps of glowing coals.

Outside, the temperature registered twenty degrees below zero. Inside, water came neither from the faucets nor the toilet. Phil wiggled under the house and checked the spring-fed pipes. They were frozen. He shoved a space heater into the crawlspace and kept it on for hours—but it didn't thaw the plumbing.

"Damn! I'm going to have to dig outside, near the spring," he told me. "Heat the supply line with a torch and hope it thaws."

Phil struggled into two pairs of long underwear, three long-sleeved t-shirts, and two wool shirts; he pulled on his trousers, two pairs of socks, and his pack boots; he wrapped a scarf around his neck and tugged two knitted hats over his head—and then he started for the door. With all those clothes, I doubted he could bend over or, if he did, feared he would fall onto his back, wiggling his arms and legs like a beetle. But he appeared confident and in good spirits as he waddled outside.

He tossed some tools into the back of the pickup, jumped in, and turned the key. Nothing happened. Trudging back in, he called a garage in town. The mechanic didn't seem to believe we didn't own an engine heater. "What's an engine heater?" Phil asked him. "And how does it work?"

After saying how we should have *prepared* for this cold snap, the mechanic took pity on Phil and explained how to drape tarps over the rig for insulation and set a heater underneath. So Phil pulled the space heater from under the house and put it under the pickup, then gathered his tools and toddled up Rosebud Creek a quarter-mile to the spring box, where he began to dig. On his first stab at the ground, the shovel clanged off the soil. With no snow to hold in warmth, the ground had frozen to the hardness of steel.

"Well, that's an interesting complication," I said when he came back in the house to warm up. "What can we do?"

"Heat the ground, build bonfires above the pipes."

"And if that doesn't work, we don't have water."

"We can use water from the creek. It didn't freeze solid. We'll boil it for drinking and heat it for sponge baths. We can flush the toilets with it, too." Phil was born hopeful. "Get out our big pots, and I'll start bringing in the water."

"It's like we're in a Laura Ingalls Wilder novel," I said. We were reading her books at the time, and sharing the adventures and hardships of Laura's pioneering family helped us get through our own adversities. I suddenly felt the energy of an adventure. I think Phil did, too, or he wouldn't have attempted his Operation Water Recovery plan over the next two months.

In one stage of the plan, Phil kept Rosebud Creek open by chopping a hole in it every day so we could fill the buckets and water the horses; in another, he placed his burn piles close to the house in an attempt to thaw the underground pipes. After the earth beneath the fires thawed, he dug at it with a steel bar, a shovel, and a mattock. After a month, however, he had managed to dig only three deep, widely-spaced test holes in his search for the house's supply line. Eventually, he exposed one tiny section of an iron pipe so old that it had probably been laid by Kennewick Man. It was as holey as a sieve and took a doglegged jog toward Rosebud Creek before angling away. Yet no matter how much he torched the exposed pipe, we couldn't get water. The whole line was frozen.

Meanwhile, the temperature continued to fall. It never rose above five degrees and often dipped to twenty-seven below. Phil got up in the middle of the night to feed the stove. To keep out the cold I tacked towels on the windows, where they froze to the glass. We developed patterns of life similar to our ancestors—getting through one day at a time. (Neighbors drove by slowly, probably to see if smoke still rose from our chimney. We suspected they'd step in if they thought we needed help, but otherwise wouldn't intrude.) By February we had endured six weeks without water. And all we could do was wait for the spring thaw.

Surviving winter fell into a rhythm. Pots or buckets of water always sat on the stove for washing, near the toilet for flushing, and by the bathtub for bathing. We "showered" by taking turns pouring warm water over each other in the tub. Somehow the house stayed clean and meals got cooked. Eventually, the truck warmed enough to make a few trips to town, but we couldn't afford an engine heater, so at night the blankets stayed draped over the truck and the heater turned on underneath.

Then one morning, after two months without running water, we woke to the sound of splashing. Blessed water was running through open faucets! Later that spring, Phil would have to dig up and repair the broken pipes, but this would do for now.

As it turned out, many other families had lost their water during the cold snap, one of the longest around here in anyone's memory. For us, it was another obstacle to overcome in our new life. In fact, we were a little sad when it was over—especially those wonderful showers.

Calving Season

It was February midnight and Phil sloshed in from his last check of the evening. "Kristy, wake up." He shook me until I sat up in bed and looked at him in dismay. "I have to pull a calf from a heifer—you want to help?"

This was a new aspect to raising cows I hadn't anticipated. Why couldn't heifers have babies on their own like animals in the wild? Heck, with all due respect to the women in my family, young and old, they shot babies out like toaster Pop Tarts. Besides, what did we know about helping a heifer have her baby? I wasn't crazy about the idea.

"This isn't good, Phil," I said, whining as much as possible. "Why can't we just wait and see if she has it on her own? I'm sure she doesn't want us poking around her…uh…area." I gave him my *special* scowl. "Besides, do you know how to do this?"

"I've watched Bard and Jeff," Phil said, referring to two neighboring ranchers, as though that would reassure me. "This is her first baby, and sometimes the heifer is too small or the calf too big. They told me to wait about two hours after we see a bubble coming out her backend. But she's taking too long."

Still, was this something I wanted to do? It was okay for cows to wander around the ranch like in some pastoral scene from a Currier & Ives print, but now it seemed we were going to get ourselves covered in cow muck.

"It's been two and a half hours," Phil said. "If we don't help, she or the calf might die."

Die. That word had an electrifying affect. Because I couldn't stand to see anything suffer, the word now meant we had no choice. "Okay," I said. "Then let's do it."

"Better get on extra gear. It's snowing like a son-of-a-gun out there."

I donned a new Carhart one-piece suit over a turtleneck and long johns, then slipped on my packs. Grabbing my wool hat and gloves, I followed Phil out into the swirling snow.

After parking the pickup so the headlights shone into the pen, we moved carefully among the twenty small heifers and tried to single out the one calving. Even with their backs covered in snow, she was easy to spot. She waddled; her arched tail switched back and forth, and a large red opaque bubble stuck out from her hind end. Clearly, she was in distress. Heifers are high-strung on their best days, but Phil had laid the groundwork for gentling ours. Every day when he brought them hay, he calmly strolled among them, scratching their heads and backs. But they still didn't like to be cornered or caught.

This time, however, she had no choice as we trudged back and forth in the small lot, trying to drive her towards the corral. If we didn't watch our footing, we knew we'd probably disappear into one of the caverns where badgers had decided to dig to China. The treacherous holes turned the simple act of walking into an Olympic sport of jumping and dodging.

After a few maddening minutes, we managed to get her into the Powder River calving pen that Phil had recently purchased, complete with a head catch that met my standards for kindness. It worked like an elongated bottleneck. Once the cow's head shot through, two vertical panels closed, trapping the neck while leaving enough space for limited movement.

The gate clanged as Phil closed it behind him and the heifer. "You run the catch from the outside," Phil said, panting. "I'll walk her in to it. Wait till she starts to put her head through, then bring the handle down to close it."

I shuddered in fear of messing up. Maybe I wouldn't pull the handle fast enough, and she'd go all the way through to rejoin her buddies. Catching her again would be difficult—she'd be testy, high tailing it away from us. On tiptoes, I stretched and grabbed the cold upright handle, wrapping my knit gloves around the rubber handgrips.

"I'm ready," I told Phil. "I can do this."

Hidden behind a solid metal panel, built to keep a cow from seeing the boogeyman that captured their heads, I peeked to see if the heifer was close, but it was risky because seeing me would scare her away from the catch.

Suddenly, a wet black nose poked through—but then quickly backed out again. She snuffled hard at the opening. Phil prodded her but she milled around, flustered. My stomach tightened.

"She's turning back towards it," Phil said. "Be ready."

Her nervous breathing got louder.

In a flash, her head lurched through. I pulled down on the handle as her shoulders slammed against the head catch with a deafening bang. She jumped around and rolled her eyes, but she was caught.

From out of the pickup Phil got a five-foot steel pole with a ratcheting handle, a short obstetric chain, and a bow-shaped aluminum gadget called a yoke. Attached to each end of the yoke was a heavy flat band, as a string is attached to a bow. He showed me how the pole fit into a round slot in the middle of the bow.

"It's a calf-puller," he said, responding to my puzzled face. "The yoke snugs up to her rear under the vaginal opening. The band sits over her back and holds up the yoke. Once the pole is in the slot, I hook the middle of the chain to the ratchet, and the ends of the chain loop around the calf's hooves that stick out the mother's vagina."

Sure enough, the bubble had burst, and shiny, wet hooves now poked out. Phil handed me his coat and rolled up his sleeves. The wind-driven snow fell so fast it coated the heifer and us. Phil grabbed up the chain.

"We have to make sure the hooves point right side up. That means the calf is coming out right—head-first rather than backwards," Phil explained while he looped the chain around the slick yellow and black hooves. "Now hand me the part with the strap."

I handed it to him, and he positioned it on the heifer. The pole came next, so I picked it up and slid it into the slot. He hooked the chain to the ratchet and pumped it a couple of times, making the chain taut. The heifer felt the tug, humped up, grunted, and had a contraction.

"Hold the end of the pole straight out while I ratchet," Phil said. "Each time she has a contraction I'll pull a little more and stop. I need to pull the calf only when the heifer pushes, or the umbilical might break too soon."

It's a good thing we've watched a lot of doctor shows on television, I reasoned. This *can't* be that different from women. Except a woman knows to do the breathing thing. Although the heifer was doing a good job grunting.

Another hefty contraction came, and Phil ratcheted faster. A loud groan came from the heifer. I held the pole handle steady. Little gangly legs appeared.

"Here it comes," I whispered. "It's coming, Phil!"

At the next contraction, Phil pumped faster. The heifer let out a heart-wrenching moan and went down, her body sagging sideways to the left.

"Should she do that?" I asked. "How can the calf come out if the heifer's down?"

"Pull the end down and to the right, and we should be okay."

"What do we do now?" I dragged the pole toward me. "Can we get her up?

Phil kept jacking on the handle. Then with a squishy *whoosh*, a long, wriggling mess slid out of the heifer. "Why isn't it moving?" I said, worried about the calf's seemingly lifeless body. "Is it dead?"

Phil pulled a shorter chain from his coat pocket and quickly hooked it around the hind legs. "Help me lift it up to get the fluid from its lungs."

I grabbed part of the chain and we climbed the side of the pen, shaking the slimy ninety-pound calf up and down until clear liquid trickled from its open mouth.

"I'll hold it," Phil said, gasping, "while you get a piece of stiff grass to put up its nose—hurry!"

I hopped down, plucked a stem from a trampled bunch of rye, and snaked it carefully up the calf's nostril. Phil slowly laid the calf on the snow. "Wiggle it around in there," he said. "It'll get it to take a breath!"

Miraculously, the dark nose twitched, then sneezed and snorted, trying to get out the niggling invader. "It's alive," I yelled, sounding like Dr. Frankenstein. "It's alive!" The calf shook its head and blinked its long, snow-sprinkled eyelashes.

"You can release her mom's head so she can clean her baby," Phil said, pulling the calf to its mother. He caught his breath and watched the heifer lick her newborn. "I think we did a good job." And we had done it ourselves.

Cow Innards

When it came to calving, we sometimes found ourselves facing something too big for us to handle alone. Then it was time to call Bard Culpepper, the irascible cowboy who worked at the ranch next door and who had taught Phil much of what he now knew about cows. On one such day, Phil paced the kitchen as he spoke on the phone. "Hey Bard," he said, swinging the twelve-foot phone cord. "I have a cow with something flopping around on her back end. It's covered with stuff as thick as my arm. Also, she gets up, lies down, and acts bothered."

"Fur how long?"

"Since this morning."

"Git 'er in. Ah'm comin'."

Ten minutes later Phil and I pushed the black cow along the highway bar pit to a corral a half-mile away. It was slow going because she walked like a fat Elvis—if he'd had a gross thing dangling from his bottom. Bard showed up munching sunflower seeds. "Tryin' to quit chewin'—*agin*," he said, spitting out pieces of shells. "Okay, now let's put 'er in the head catch. Ah need to see if she's got a calf in 'er." He wiggled into a plastic glove as long as an elephant's trunk and added clear goo from a squirt bottle smeared with grime and eased his arm into the vagina.

"Calf's dead an' hard," he said. "Bin theer awhal. Ah'll stick some local anesthetic in 'er jugular so's sheel sleep an' ah'll cut 'er open." If Phil's and my eyebrows had been glued together, they couldn't have shot up in better sync.

"You mean a cesarean?" Phil asked, a hint of incredulity creeping into his voice. "Won't she die?" Bard shot him a Yosemite Sam look, the handlebar drooping with disapproval. "Just wondering," Phil added quickly.

"Ain't sure. Lahkely."

Bard laid out his surgeon's paraphernalia while murmuring sweet nothings to them as if to his best girl, and with tenderness he laid them on a plaid shirt with holes in it the size of cantaloupes. Dried brown globs connected the instruments along with hairs, bits of pills, and something resembling snail slime.

"Shouldn't we boil something?" Phil said. "Kristy could go to the house and scrub your instruments with bleach." He picked up the single unit of scalpel-needle-scissors. "She could also bring back some Gardener's soap, towels, fingernail brush, Q-tips, Bee's Knees hand lotion. Matter of fact, I could go with her. Okay then. Good luck. Stop by for a Vanilla Chai espresso when you're done."

"Yur helpin'," Bard said, stuffing a handful of sunflower seeds in his mouth. "The both o' yew."

Resigned, we hovered anxiously, watching Bard give the shot of anesthetic. The cow meandered around the corral for three minutes before she collapsed. An eruption of dirt rose around her, then cascaded onto her body. The ground was dry for late April, so each step we took produced waves of powder floating like the dry ice in *Abbott and Costello Meet the Wolfman.*

Bard's eye's twinkled at us, his mood lifting as he knelt next to his patient's mountain-shaped belly.

"Heh-heh-heh," he said. "It is our good fortoone she went down on 'er raht side cause weel open 'er on the left. See, when the yewtrus is full with a calf in it, the yewtrus ends up on the left side. Normally it's on the raht side. Easy as pie. Now ah'll put a few deadnin' shots of Lidocaine aroun' whar ah'll cut." From his pocket he pulled out a new plastic-capped needle and loaded it with fluid from a rubber-tipped bottle. He pricked the cow five times in a foot wide circle. Five minutes passed as we waited. "Hand me mah knife." The glued wad of operating implements crackled apart like a sourdough's hardtack as I worked at separating the mass. Bard held out his hand like Dr. Kildare.

"This century, mebbe?"

With the scalpel he sliced a foot-long incision in the hide, another slice into the muscles, then another in the peritoneal cavity. Before the last cut into the uterus, an expanding bulk pushed energetically under the elastic barrier of membrane. Without warning, organs began spilling out. Fat round ones. Long skinny ones. Some red and others white but most of them blue-veined.

An uncharacteristic "Eeek!" escaped Bard's lips along with a couple of seeds. "Need hep heer," he shouted, galvanizing Phil and me into action. In our haste to assist, we tripped over Bard, each other, and cow innards as Bard snapped out orders.

"Grab this! Hold onto thet! Push hard! Stan' back!"

The three of us wrestled with entrails, forcing them back into the incision while keeping a clear path for Bard to cut open the uterus.

"Aha! Jest as ah thought," he said, puffing. "Phil—grab the calf's leg an' pull slow-like." Just then I spotted the cord disappearing into the cow's rear as they began muscling out the dead calf. "Is that thing supposed to go back inside like that?" I asked. "It's unhygienic."

"*Thang*?" he said. " Oh—*thet*. Wal, weel bring it raht on through."

The two men grunted and strained, which is what the cow should have done originally, until a calf slowly emerged, crooked, twisted, and atrophied with its legs locked and its body frozen in a fetal position. Shrunken facial skin exposed teeth looking like rows of corn. It resembled something in a jar at a circus sideshow. Fastened to it, now much cleaner after having passed through the cow's insides, was the cord. Phil set the calf and its cord aside. At that moment, the cow's ear twitched. A panicky look flitted across Bard's face.

"Quick! Han' me thet curved needle an' thread. Thar for stitchin' up the inner layers—no, wait. First sprinkle thet antibiotic powder in thar." I daintily tapped some over the cavernous opening. "No, no, no. Give it to me—we ain't got all day."

He grabbed the box and showered the gash with roundhouse sweeps. Three or four shakes of the antibiotic and the black cow turned white. So did we.

"Now the yewtrus boluses—we'll stick a few in 'er heer an' thar. Cain't ever have too many antibiotics." From another pocket Bard drew out a box, and in the spirit of the Easter Bunny hid six or eight boluses, each the size of a gerbil's head, in strategic spots inside the cavity.

"*Now* the needle an' cat gut," he whispered, perched a nose-length away from the inner incision of the uterus. He quickly punctured then pulled. Each time he spoke, hairs from his moustache, long and sweeping, barely escaped the loop. A vein bulged on his forehead. His cowboy hat fell off, revealing four hairs lifted straight up in the breeze.

After a frenzied stitching through all the layers—all of them accompanied by mumblings, screeches, and a flutter of sunflower shells landing both inside and outside the wound—he tied the finishing knot of umbilical tape with a flourish.

"One last roun' of insurance," he announced, digging in his tackle box and bringing out a brown bottle and a needle gun. "LA-200!" He reverently filled the glass part of the needle gun with the liquid. "This stuff's the rancher's savin' grace. Goes in the muscle, another antibiotic fur good measure." He stuck the cow in the side of her neck, behind her shoulder, and on her hip.

Now done with his work, he settled back against the cow that still slept, although she jerked occasionally. Contentment flowed across his face. Phil and I were spent, ragged from our first cesarean.

"Bet yew-all thought ah wus in trouble back theer," Bard said with a chuckle. "Jest funnin' with yew. Niver wus a problem. Had it under control the whole time. Yew needed to git a taste o' how it kin be in a emergency." He got up to go. "Wahl. It's bin reel. Let me know if she dies."

The cow got up in a half-hour started eating hay, and in a few months we could barely see a scar. We called Bard to give him the news.

"Really?" He sounded surprised. "Uh—ah mean—ah wusn't a bit worried."

Branding Time

I seized the phone on the second ring."I'm at the Gallagher ranch," Phil said from the other end. "They stopped me on the highway and invited us to their branding tomorrow."

Phil's curiosity about all things ranchy was growing. He was spending more time with cows and less with his leatherwork, metamorphosing from artisan to rancher. I saw this branding invitation as another step. "But we don't know how to do whatever it is ranchers do to their cows."

"I know," he said. "But it would be fun!"

Well, maybe it *would* be interesting to see them work close-up. Besides, I didn't want to be left behind. When we married, I vowed to work together so we wouldn't grow apart. I noticed that most of the ranch women worked alongside their men, so if Phil leaned in that direction, then so would I.

The next morning as we slowed down near the Gallagher ranch, I heard the red-winged blackbirds sing their *Thweedly yeep! Thweedly yeep!* outside our pickup window. More than fifteen other pickups, half of them attached to horse trailers and parked haphazardly, lined each side of the highway. Children dressed like tiny cowboys and cowgirls, complete with big hats, darted out from between the trailers and crossed the narrow road. A massive dust cloud told us where the corral was. We parked and walked over. Bodies perched on a skinny pole fence materialized out of the floating grime. They howdied as we passed deeper into the inner sanctum where there clustered more humans. Dogs colored with reds, browns, blacks, and whites wove between Levi legs, including ours. Cows and calves, already separated from one another, bawled continuously.

"Phil and Kristy! Over here!" yelled Jeff Gallagher, tall and skinny and holding the reins of a jaunty Pinto gelding. "Watch out ever'body. Here come the hippies!"

Our neighbors got a kick out of teasing us. I figured out early on that it was their way of accepting us. I'd heard it sometimes took forty years for that acceptance to happen. Jeff was the spitting image of a young John Wayne. An older version of the same actor sauntered over—Jeff's dad, Shane. "Hi, kids," he said, holding out a jug of Century Club bourbon to Jeff, who took a whopping gulp.

Jeff's eyebrows asked us if we wanted any. It was eight in the morning, so my stomach said no. Phil also declined. I was too shy to ask how they drink with those big wads of chew stuffed in their lips.

"What are our jobs, Jeff?" Phil asked. "What can we do?"

"You'll be ropin'," Jeff said with a deadpan expression. "You can rope can'tcha?" Then he laughed at his own joke. So did we, although once again I thought, What are we doing here?

"Aw, Kristy, don't get all twitterpated now," Jeff said, seeming to read my mind. "Why don't you go on over to the ladies and say hi."

As the guys started talking about the fine points of branding, I wandered over to Amy, Jeff's wife. She had golden hair, a fresh face, a natural beauty, and a vivacious personality. "We're the ground crew," she explained as we squatted together on a wide chunk of log.

She saw me staring at four cowboys tightening the cinches on their saddled horses. "One rider throws for the head first," Amy explained. "Then his partner throws a sideways loop for the hind legs, hoping the calf steps into it. When they have at least one backleg and the head, they drag it to the fire."

The four riders mounted up. A young fellow in the corral opened a gate and let in twenty calves. Two riders paired off and headed to one end of the corral, checking their rope loops as they moseyed along.

"That's where we come in," Amy explained. "Jump on the calf, flip it on its side, and move the head rope around to the front legs. It's not good to keep the head in a loop because it might choke the calf. Then we give it shots for diseases, castrate it if it's a bull, notch its ear, brand it, burn the horns, and maybe cut a wattle under the chin."

"A wattle?"

"A strip of skin left attached like a flap for identification, a sign of ownership. Makes it easier to tell from a distance if it's your cow. Ranchers cut the skin in different ways so it hangs in distinctive folds or odd shapes."

As she spoke, she filled a huge syringe whose needle resembled a short nail. "The guys take turns roping and working on the ground. They usually notch, tag, castrate, and brand. A few of the women rope, but not many."

Just then, Jeff threw a loop and caught the calf's head while another young man named Charlie got a back foot. Jeff dragged the calf to us while Charlie followed. As they stretched the calf between their two horses, two men flipped the calf over and switched the head rope to the front legs. Then the ground crew sprung into action.

Amy and her younger sister, Tess, crouched by the calf and stuck in their needles—one in the neck muscle and the other under the skin. Jeff's uncle Noel castrated the calf. Shane brought a hot iron down to the calf's hide, and with the smell of burning hair and skin came the pain that made the calf howl and thrust out his tongue. At the same time, a stout cowboy gouged a hot iron into the two small horn buds on each side of the calf's head. I felt sick.

After three hours, six ropers and as many as ten people on the ground had worked more than seventy calves. During that time, I kept my feelings to myself, afraid of being "branded" an outsider, of losing the acceptance that we'd already gained.

When the Gallagher family invited the entire crew to lunch, a common practice among hospitable ranchers, I was still so disturbed by what I'd seen that I hunkered down with my plate of food in a corner of the house. Eventually, Shane came over and eased himself down on a footstool near me.

"Didn't care for it, huh?" His smile was kind. He didn't seem like someone who enjoyed torturing animals. But I couldn't answer, couldn't tell him I thought it was barbaric. It helped that my mouth was full of potato salad.

"The cost of a veterinarian would run too high," Shane said, "so we've been taught how to do this on our own by our fathers and grandfathers. It may not look like it, but we're careful. Each generation refines its techniques, and we rarely lose a calf."

"It hurts them."

"Yes, it does, but only for a short while. Then they get with their mamas, have a good meal, lie down, and sleep. That's healing."

"I love to see them running in little packs," I said, "with their tails in the air, like flying monkeys in the *Wizard of Oz*."

"That'll take about a week," he assured me. "Then you'll see it again." He patted my arm and then left.

I decided I'd probably never like brandings. But, like Dorothy in the Emerald City, I'd never taken a peek behind the curtain before, had never seen the other side. Now that I had, I realized that somebody had to do the dirty work if I was going to eat hamburger or prime rib. In fact, if Phil kept getting involved ever more deeply in this life, we'd soon be doing the same thing ourselves.

Horseback Riding

Our first adventure with horses began hundreds of miles away from Izee, in the Oregon City Elks Lodge Bar over a few dozen drinks, with Dad bragging to a fellow named Reese Quintin about the ranch and mentioning that during deer season he needed riders to push the deer to his guests who'd be hunting there. Reese said that if he could hunt, too, he'd bring his horses and help. So on the evening before opening day, Reese arrived at the old ranch house, and Phil—eager to start riding, though he'd never ridden much—showed up before dawn the next morning.

After hasty introductions, Phil sat on a rickety chair and waited as Reese snatched a half-full bottle of Hood River vodka out of the freezer and splashed some into his morning coffee. He looked Phil over. "C'mon, Phil," he said, "I brought a horse for you. My grandkids walk under his belly." In a quick gulp, he downed the potent brew, wiped his leathery chin, and ambled out to the pole barn. Phil followed like a puppy.

In the barn, one light bulb exposed the massive and cobwebby pine logs cut long ago from the ranch's timber. The smells of horseflesh, molasses oats, and fresh hay filled the chilly air. Reese grabbed a matted currycomb and slapped it into Phil's hand. Phil kept an eye on Reese while dragging the brush over the quivering hide of a tiny mare named Sheila. Reese gathered bridles off thick nails and slid blankets and saddles from horse-chewed stalls. He saddled Sheila while Phil groomed the other horse, a gelding named Sugarpuss. If anyone could call it a horse. He resembled an elephant. Probably some mix-up during mating season near a zoo.

Reese threw a saddle on Sugarpuss and led both horses outside, where Phil decided to show manly initiative and got on Sheila. "No son," Reese told him. "Here's yours." He nodded toward the elephantine gelding.

"That can't be right, Mr. Quintin," Phil said, trying not to sound petulant. "You'd ride the bigger horse, right?"

"Nope. Sugarpuss is too slow and gentle." The words *slow* and *gentle* gave Phil the impetus to slide off Sheila. With the mutant gelding's stirrup at eye level, Phil had to jump to grab the horn. Climbing leather, his feet dangling in the air, he wiggled his way up to the saddle. "Okay," Phil said, finally settling in the saddle. "But if you change your mind, let me know."

Reese grabbed the saddle horn, swung onto his little mare, and began trotting off as Sheila shook her head and expelled gas. "Remember, Phil," Reese yelled over his shoulder, "a farting horse never tires. A farting man is the man to hire."

On the ride down the driveway, fog swirled around both riders. Phil relaxed and began enjoying the ride. "I'm an old cowhand," he hummed, "from the Rio Grande."

"We'll turn off the road and go straight up the mountain," Reese said, obviously familiar with this kind of terrain. "And don't you worry—that horse will take you anywhere."

He turned off the road and towards the creek at the base of the hill. Phil nudged Sugarpuss forward. But as Reese reached the water, Sheila suddenly fell to her knees and sent Reese hurtling over her head. He landed on all fours, then leaped up, flashing a sheepish smile. Phil turned Sugarpuss towards home.

"Aw, c'mon now, Phil—don't let that bother you," Reese shouted, getting back on Sheila. "She just tripped, is all. Don't fret!" Chuckling, he headed the mare up the mountain. Phil trailed behind but was ready to jump off at a moment's notice.

They climbed the hill in switchbacks, and at a narrow game trail near the top, Reese told Phil to ride north up the ridge towards Old Car Draw, where the hunters' stands were. Then Reese continued climbing and left Phil alone.

For Phil, the only sound was the gelding's footfalls clumping along the path. An unexpected, sweet sense of harmony with life washed through him. The world looked different from horseback. His senses sharpened. He saw the sun lighten Mahogany

Mountain. As Sugarpuss halted at a steep gully filled with granddaddy junipers, a loud whooshing noise came from above. It grew louder until, suddenly, a red-tailed hawk blasted by Phil at eye level. The songs of migrating finches, robins, and blue birds erupted from the juniper's gnarled branches. That enchanted moment had a profound impact on Phil, who once again felt forever transformed.

But my first riding experience wasn't as Zen-like. I did *not* become one with the horse. It happened a couple of days after Phil's epiphany. With three fat bucks—Dad's and his guests'—hanging in the shed, it was time to go back to work. Phil coaxed me to ride with him and Reese to round up Dad's stray cows from the forest.

"The horses are loaded," Reese said, jumping into Dad's '56 stock truck. "Hop in, kids!" I slid in the middle.

"You'll love it, Kristy," Phil whispered to me, trying to put a good light on my pending death. "Reese is a good old boy."

Good? At what? Fixing shattered bones when I'm pitched off my horse onto a pile of knife-edged rocks?

As I mentally tried out a peaceful mantra I'd remembered from the *Kung Fu* TV show, we drove east on the highway to the Malheur National Forest. Reese turned onto the 6370 road while his raspy voice droned on about his cement business and his son the rodeo rider, about growing up in Pendleton and hunting in Wallowa County's Chesnimnus country. I tried to be polite, but my mind was on unclenching my sphincter and ignoring my bad-tempered bowels. After one particularly noisy intestinal gripe, Reese glanced at me. "What, hon?"

Phil calmly patted my knee. I wanted to grab his ear and twist it like his mama never did. Being scared made me grumpy.

"Pint-size," Reese said to me as he backed the truck up against a high bank near a sign that said Bunton Hollow. "Phil said you've ridden Joe, keerrect?"

"Uhhh…well…ridden isn't the word so much as…*sat*." I told him. "I *sat* on him during our first visit here. Dad held the reins." I was talking to air because Reese and Phil had already scooted out, opened the truck gate, and unloaded the horses. Phil, seasoned from his one-day ride, hopped on his horse like Roy Rogers. Reese held Joe.

I hoped the horse couldn't see the horror in my eyes. If it was time, I wasn't ready. I needed to go home and do…stuff. In fact, I was sure that spot between my eyebrows needed tweezed. Suddenly, I felt myself lifted up and plopped down onto Joe's back.

"There you go, sweet pea," said Reese, handing me the reins. "Next time you'll get up there yourself. You'll see."

Reese mounted Sheila, and we began walking too quickly along the road. But because I didn't die immediately, my confidence grew until I thought, Hey, I'm riding a horse! This is easy. I'm Annie Oakley.

But then Reese turned Sheila hard to the right and began climbing a steep, rocky slope. Joe seemed to like the idea and lurched upward. My stomach stayed on the road. I closed my eyes. Our horses scrambled for footing on loose rocks. Behind me I saw the *tops* of old-growth Ponderosa pines. Tumbling down the mountain seemed to be a real possibility. "Phil, I'm not happy here," I shouted, "so I'll get off and walk."

"Kristy," Phil said in his best here-I-go-having-to-humor-her-again voice. "There's only this skinny deer trail. Cowboy up."

I was preparing to spit out a righteous, bitchy retort when we hit the ridge, where the trail flattened. Phil and Reese climbed down from their horses. "I'll check the taillights," Reese said, glancing at me. "Just thought you should know, pipsqueak." He led his horse toward a dense bush.

Phil hung back with me. "Okay, I'll bite." I said, finding it hard to sulk. "Why would a bush be called a *taillight*?"

When Reese came back, Phil, now a good old boy himself, repeated my question to him. Both men laughed so hard I thought they would throw up. Miffed, I tried to dismount gracefully, but Joe's legs seemed to have grown longer since I first climbed into the saddle, and I fell to the ground. That started a new fit of hilarity. Reese, his face bright red and streaked with tears, tried to say something. But each effort brought on a choking fit. Disgusted and sitting in the dirt, I mentally searched my cuss word repertoire.

"Why muffin," Reese said at last, smiling, "you're no bigger than a pint of horse piss with the foam farted off."

Actually, I didn't get it—but I still appreciated the creativity, so I joined them in a good laugh. As it turns out, I can be a good old boy, too.

Ranch Women

Ranch women unintentionally intimidate a city-born girl like me. Brave, talented, and feisty, they are like the heroines in adventure novels. I figure it's because they were born into the life. Their mothers probably gave birth to them out in the sagebrush then tied off the umbilical cords with a strip of dirty old saddle leather—while on a weeklong cattle drive. Ranch women can castrate calves with their teeth while serving their branding crews lunch, and they can clean their houses while mending saddles, churning butter, and ironing silk neckerchiefs. Okay, those might be embellishments, but I'm not far off.

Our earliest encounter with an incredible ranch lady came when the outdoor thermometer read ten-degrees as Phil chopped firewood and I stacked it near our driveway. Suddenly the eerie, rapid clipping of hooves cut the air, and out of the icy fog burst a white cow the size of a Volkswagen. It was charging straight at us, like some bovine Hound of the Baskervilles. A horse and rider followed close on the cow's tail. Phil started to leap in front of the cow when a feminine voice rang out.

"Wouldn't do that, son. She'll just run ya down," advised the rider sweetly as she flew past, grinning at us with perfect, red, Rita Hayworth lips. "Her head's up and nothing in front will stop 'er."

Phil's mouth dropped open.

On top of the bay horse sat a stunning silver-haired cowgirl. Her small, buckskin-gloved hand brandished a braided leather whip, and with a practiced flourish she snapped it over the cow's snowy head. I wondered if I'd stepped back a century; she was so lovely that she should have been riding sidesaddle and wearing a velvet hat with a peacock feather.

Abruptly, the startled cow tweaked her course and hurtled down the highway. The anonymous equestrian waved and disappeared, following her charge.

This eye-popping episode prompted me to ask around about her. Sure enough, neighbors knew the mysterious rider. I found that people, mostly dreamy-eyed men, chatted eagerly about her.

"Oh, that 'ud be Lark Chandler," one old-timer told me. "As a girl, with two foot o' golden hair streamin' down 'er back, she'd jump into a pen full o' riled yearlin's crackin' that whip. Those animals quickly danced to 'er tune, and she displayed nary a scratch."

"Yep," said another admirer. "That gal rode like a maniac in two risky cross-country races. Came in first in one and third in another. The other riders? All fellas. Nope, just not many like her, even in eastern Oregon."

This description also fit Phoebe, a pocket-sized redhead and the only offspring of the Sloans. A nurse by day, Phoebe in her spare time broke her own horses, sometimes riding flighty colts alone into the forest while looking for her cattle. Then one day a colt spooked, bucking Phoebe off and causing her to bash her head on a rock.

"I woke up disoriented as my horse grazed peacefully nearby," she said. "I crawled up on him, and he took me back to my truck. I downed a couple of beers, finished looking for cattle, pushed them into the next pasture and drove home."

Later, she learned she'd sustained a bad concussion and possible vision impairment. The next day, however, she returned to work, just like so many other eastern Oregon women.

Soon after the accident, she helped us bring in our cattle from Buck Creek. As I traveled along a ridge I spied Phoebe below me, riding hard to get around a few escaping pairs on our meadow. Next time I saw her she was on foot, and her horse was galloping downriver. I drew near and saw she'd bruised her face and torn her shirt and jeans.

"He stepped in a badger hole and tumbled head over heels tossing me off," she said, panting hard. "Not his fault. He only trained in a paddock. Can I take your horse and go catch mine?"

"Sure," I told her, grateful that I wasn't the one who'd flipped with the horse. And I was doubly thankful I didn't have to retrieve her horse, which meant galloping across the hole-pocked meadow. With a smile on her face and not a word of complaint, she caught her horse easily and finished out the gather by bringing in a dozen pairs from the hills.

On a different occasion, Phoebe, a natural daredevil, competed in a horserace at the Grant County Fair. I was there, too, but the most bravado I mustered was standing in a safe spot outside the fence rails while screaming high-pitched cheers. The riders, all cowboys except for Phoebe, bear-hugged long-muscled necks with fluttering manes as they rocketed by for five dust-swelling laps. She lost, but not by much. Undaunted, she cheerfully ended up at the beer booth with the other cowboys, who toasted her grit, although they used a more masculine term.

Not all Izee ladies, however, like manhandling sweaty horses and pestering headstrong cows. Some, like Swedish Lana, fancy keeping the home fires burning.

Once Wade, Phil, and I waited for the return of our neighbor, Rafe Anderson, manager of the Izee Ranch, in his sparkling clean ranch house kitchen while Lana—his tall, buxom wife—served us fresh cardamom bread and hot chocolate laced with cinnamon. We had settled in companionably, luxuriating in our good fortune of stopping in on Lana's baking day, when Wade's head jerked away from his mug. "Didja hear that?" He mumbled slurpily through a chocolate moustache. "Over there!" We followed his pointing finger to the refrigerator. A small whiskered nose peaked from behind the fridge at us.

"Oooh! It's the wood rat! Get that broom and hit him," bellowed Lana, listening from the pantry. "I've been trying to get it all morning."

Phil grabbed a dustpan and Wade the broom, while I issued rat-movement reports like an air traffic controller as it scampered around the kitchen. At last they thumped him. As Phil bent to scoop him into the dustpan, Lana blasted out of the pantry with a deadly-looking butcher's knife held with both hands high over her head. The moment turned into a slow motion scene from a B horror film.

The guys' faces (and mine too, no doubt) first revealed a Psycho-esque surprise—then sheer panic. As Lana swept past them and they cringed backwards, she fell to her knees and hacked the bushy tail clean off the rat.

"Hah!" she yelled, holding up her prize. "Finally got the tail for a second earring!"

I'm happy to say I never saw her wearing the tails anywhere near food at community potlucks, although I wondered later if such a fashion involved some ranch-woman ritual. I made a mental note to look up Swedish customs.

Still another remarkable woman was the stately Louise Hoffsted. Louise, her husband Ernst, and their three teenage daughters—Sara, Mia, and Jill—owned a ranch on the southeast end of Izee. One year Phil and I helped them gather their cows on the forest permit. After unloading the horses and saddling up, the young girls silently melted into the forest like mountain quail scattering in opposite directions.

"Kristy can follow behind me," Louise said.

So Phil decided to tag along with Ernst, and I lost my safety net (Phil) who would let me get mad if I got scared. Now I had to act civilized and be polite. This made me fume inside. Murmuring salty expletives as Louise headed downhill on a precipitous trail leading deeper into the pines and firs, I mounted Bimbo on the fly, almost sliding off the other side.

My disgruntled mood softened as I watched the charming vision of this middle-aged woman riding in front of me with her lush salt-and-pepper hair pinned in a chic French twist. Her faultless posture mesmerized me. Louise's horse moved like a supermodel, hooves seeming to float above the trail. What's more, as Louise trotted, her left arm rose horizontally and her pinky finger arched in a tiny, jaunty curve similar to a ballerina balancing during a pirouette. The sight was a kinetic poem. I hardly noticed my crushing grip on the saddle horn or the uncontrollable flopping of my body on the horse.

Every minute or so Louise would look back, and I would whip my hands off the horn and hold only the reins. For some reason it was important for her to believe not only that I could handle my horse, but also that I found it a snap to ride the treacherous path we were following.

We traveled for an hour and never found a cow, though she wasn't concerned. She even flashed me a cheery grin as we pulled up to their horse trailer.

"Good ride, huh?" she said. "Kristy, you sit on a horse as if you were born and raised here."

My laugh was a tad too hearty because I felt slightly remorseful at the deception involving the saddle horn.

"You laugh," she added, "but lots of these ranch ladies came from the city as young women, too. Many of us learned ranching after we moved here."

My lingering smile vanished. Oh, shoot—there went my excuse.

Deer Hunt

Because I was trying to make myself into a ranch woman, I decided to kill a buck. Ranch women do these things. When we first moved here, for example, Wade mentioned to our Native American stagecoach lady ("mail deliverer" to urban folk) that he'd killed a duck—he happened to be holding it at the time—but didn't know how to clean it. With a crumpled hand-rolled cigarette hanging from her mustached lip, she snatched the duck from Wade, gutted it, and plucked it so fast that feathers and down drifted in the air. Then she drove away, waving goodbye out the window with a hand swathed in blood and feathers. That's what I was up against.

Phil had already stalked, killed, dragged, and dressed two bucks, then cut them up and wrapped the meat for the freezer. The hippie I'd married seemed to have turned into a horseman-hunter guy. Who knew he had this latent urge? Heck, he used to rescue disoriented tree frogs from the house and set them free outside. Anyhow, now it was my turn to hunt, though two deer seasons passed before I actually did it.

During both seasons I eased into it by riding on Joe's knobby back and pushing deer to the hunters on stand. The arthritic old horse made me feel safe as long as we only plodded the deer trails, but I had to face the reality of death whenever the crack of a rifle from over the hill told me someone had shot his deer.

My next step was staring into the glazed eyes of the dead deer. It's rough seeing them that way, but I still *oohed* and *aahed* as the hunters' fresh kills arrived in the pickup bed, the bucks' stiff legs pointing heavenward and waving with each bump in the road.

At the end of the third season, the family's hunters returned to the west side with their deer heads and wrapped carcasses, but Phil had yet to fill his tag. Squelching my feminine side, I told Phil I would kill a buck.

"This will be perfect," he said, so excited he was trying not to jump up and down. He never dreamed I'd ever want to shoot anything. "It's just the two of us, so you won't be under any pressure. We'll hunt Buck Creek. Hell, there must have been a hundred bucks up there!"

At 5:30 on the morning of the hunt, I rolled over in bed and nudged the bulk beside me. "Phil."

"Mumfle shlurg rifleech."

"Aren't we supposed to be up and killing something?" I poked once more, then got up and started coffee and bacon.

"It's a great day, my little hunter-woman," Phil said, grinning as he sat down to breakfast. "I'm gonna have you shoot the .308 Remington. It has a short barrel and isn't too heavy. You'll feel a kick but won't notice it in the excitement. I'll carry my Sako just in case."

I glanced out the kitchen window that faces south towards Buck Creek. Dawn seemed a couple of blinks away as the hills began taking shape.

"We'll take the pickup to the base of the slope and climb to the ridge," he explained. "I'll leave you under that spidery, low-branched juniper."

"You'll *leave* me?" I started hiccupping. "Shouldn't you be there to, you know, talk me through it? Wipe my brow? Shoot the buck yourself? I don't even know if I can do it. In fact, there are a darn lot of *if's* here, my friend." But Phil just grinned and took a bite of toast.

A half hour later we were hiking up the hill, our rifles hanging from our shoulders and banging against our hips. When we stopped for breath, Phil whispered one-line pep talks, such as, "You'll be fine, you won't panic," or "No, you won't shoot me accidentally." That last one seemed important.

"We need to be quiet," he said, panting and leaning toward my ear. "We might spook the deer." I nodded, my mouth refusing to let any saliva form. It must have been around 7:30 when we reached the top. The sky was a perfect blue. The air was still. I heard a car traveling the highway perhaps two miles away. A magpie squawked at us from the juniper tree where I would hunker. Phil led me beneath it, sat me down next to a rotted log, and gave his last-minute instructions. He'd acquired lots of useful knowledge from both Dad and Reese Quintin, both of whom had hunted since before they were teenagers.

"Okay," Phil whispered, "I'll walk back down the hill behind us." He pointed west, where our ridge dropped into a ravine that ran parallel to the meadow. "I'll skirt around the hill below you and walk east to drive the deer in front of me. They'll go by you just underneath this ridge. A buck will come last in the group. He'll probably give you a nice broadside shot because they'll be traveling around the base of the hill, away from me. Wait for your shot. Aim at the shoulder." Once again he took me through the gun basics. During yesterday's practice I'd shot on target. But today was not practicing—it was killing.

"You'll do great," he said, kissing my forehead. Then he turned and left.

I was alone.

I tried to stay focused. A bullet waited in the chamber, and the rifle rested on my knee. I scooted farther under the tree. After a nail-biting half-hour passed, I finally heard animals breathing hard and running on loose gravel. Eight deer ran below me at a good clip. The last one was a buck. Slowly I brought my rifle up, snuggled the stock against my cheek, and took a bead on the buck's shoulder. My heart hammered against my ribs. I squeezed the trigger.

The recoil jolted me backwards, and the next moment found me gazing skyward with my rifle tangled in the juniper branches overhead. Hurriedly, I looked towards where the buck had been standing. He was gone.

Didn't I hit him? I thought. *Did I get buck fever? Why did this juniper grab me?* Then the buck magically appeared on the ridge, seeming to offer another broadside shot. Was this the same buck? He didn't look hurt. I jerked my rifle free, jacked in another shell, aimed and squeezed the trigger. This time I held my ground better. The recoil only knocked me back against the log. Again I looked for the buck. But again he was gone. I began to wonder if I'd entered a netherworld where I imagined a buck and then made it disappear. Then the real world returned with a blast from Phil's Sako.

“DOWN HERE!” he shouted.

I struggled up from my mulchy nest, limped on crampy legs to the south side of the hill, and peeked into the steep gully. Halfway down, Phil knelt, frantically sifting dirt with one hand while holding half of his glasses up to one eye with the other. I slid down and scooted over to him.

“Heard your shots,” he told me. “Saw a buck come into the ravine. Humped up, head down. I shot and my glasses busted in half. Don’t know if I got him.”

Kneeling beside him, I helped search, and a minute later we found it. Because both of us were nearly legally blind without glasses—though I wore contacts—he had to hold both lenses to his eyes to navigate. I picked up his rifle, and we stepped lightly over the loose topsoil and down the slope to the ravine. Twice I fell, sending marble-sized rocks tumbling downward as a warning to all wild things.

At the bottom lay the buck. He looked as though he’d folded his legs, lowered his head, and died.

“I never hit him,” Phil said, checking the entry wounds. “Two shots—and they’re both yours.” He turned towards me. “Good job, Kristy!”

Yeah, I guess. I looked at the animal whose life I had taken because I aspired to be a ranch woman. Yet this didn’t give me an ounce of satisfaction—just regret. Oh, I knew that his days were numbered and he had a darn nice rack, that I was a meat eater and he would provide for the coming year. But I didn’t have to be the one who counted coup. Still, I knew my responsibility.

As in days of old, I silently asked his forgiveness and gave him my thanks.

Rescued Animals

Unlike the methodical plotting required for a deer hunt, death on a ranch often arrives accidentally, sneaking in from nowhere and hitting hard. But like a child unable to accept it, I have a crazy notion to try to save all living things from suffering. I know—it sounds…*lofty*. Still, situations arise in which animals need rescuing.

One day, for example, while jogging along Rosebud Creek I spotted a coyote sitting close to the road. My yelling and jumping up and down finally scared it off, but it had obviously lingered for a reason. Sure enough, hidden in the tall rye grass lay a fawn, curled up and sleeping. I raced home and brought back Phil to show him the adorable fawn. We knew not to touch it. Except that's exactly what Phil did because he sensed something wasn't right.

Kneeling next to the fawn, he gently stroked its head. "It's too calm," he said, feeling along the spotted flanks. "That's odd." Gently lifting a back leg, he saw a long, open wound in the fawn's stomach. The white belly fur contrasted starkly with the red gash.

"Damn!" I said, heart-sick. "I stopped the coyote from killing it?"

"Probably. It's in shock. Get the rifle out of the truck, please."

Cussing the coyote for finding the scentless fawn, I grabbed the .22 and took it to Phil. We sat on each side of the fawn, stroking its head while telling it we were sorry, though it's a mystery whether the fawn in its last moments of life heard us apologizing and sniffing back tears. Then I shut myself in the pickup and plugged my ears. But the muffled rifle shot still echoed across Rosebud.

Another time, the coyotes succeeded with a cow up Cemetery Draw. Because cows occasionally calve in remote places, leaving themselves and their newborns vulnerable, the Cemetery calving lot contained a number of hidey-holes. One day as we drove the lot to check the herd, under a low-branching juniper tree we saw a cow lying with her back downhill. She looked dead. Phil parked nearby, scaring up scavenging magpies. The cow heard the commotion and whipped her head up. Her eyes were wild with pain and fear.

"Phil," I whispered. "Look at her—" I couldn't finish. The horror of her condition was too much. Coyotes had chewed out all of her back-end, leaving a cavern of exposed bone, dried blood, and red tissue extending from her backbone to both back legs. We found bloody drag marks but no calf.

"They attacked while she was calving," Phil said. "She couldn't get up."

"What can we do for her?"

Phil just shook his head. And once again, I brought him the rifle and then retreated to the truck.

But it isn't always a predator that causes suffering and death. On one sunny May day, for example, Phil's parents came from Portland with their two-year-old bay stallion. A nearby neighbor offered to turn the stallion into a gelding. Phil's dad decided it was cheaper than hiring a veterinarian. Phil's mom and I had a bad feeling about it, but no one asked our opinion. The men chose to perform the castration behind the house on the grassy bank of Rosebud Creek. In spite of the charming setting, it gave the impression of a seedy backroom abortion.

Inside the house, Phil's mom watched out the window while I tried to ignore what was going on outside. "They've roped him," she reported, "and now he's down, and they're cutting, but he's flailing around!"

Unable to tune her out, I wished she'd wash dishes or bake cookies.

"They're done," she said. "He's trying to get up. He's shaky—oh no! He's jumping around. They're trying to calm him down."

Stepping to the window, I saw the men gripping the ropes, trying to steady the terrified horse. For a brief moment he appeared to be okay. But then, without warning, he staggered forward and fell down, his body convulsing with spasms. He thrashed on the ground, apparently in shock, until he finally lay still. The men stood helpless, staring in disbelief. An hour earlier, this innocent horse with a sweet-tempered personality had been romping around the pasture—and now he was dead.

There are so many sad cases like the fawn, the cow, and the horse that it's easy to overlook the occasions when we've saved creatures, such as the time Phil rode his favorite old horse, Sandy, to gather the yearling steers that had scattered across the forest permit. The August day turned hot and sultry, probably too much for a horse of Sandy's years working steep hills and gullies running after frisky, young yearlings.

Then, without warning, Sandy fell, panting hard and turning over onto his side. Phil jumped off, released the cinch, and pulled off the saddle. For a half-hour he frantically fanned his cowboy hat over Sandy's head. The big sorrel eventually recovered his strength, rolled onto his chest, and stood on wobbly legs. Phil carefully loaded him into the horse trailer and drove home.

Another fortunate recovery happened during calving season, when we found a pregnant cow unable to rise. Her head was up, but she refused to stand. Twice we gave her calcium, once intravenously and once injected into the muscle, but it had no effect. Neither did yelling, nudging her from horseback, and poking her with a stick; the cow stayed grounded. So we placed a metal-paneled cage around her to protect her water and hay, and every day Phil took the caterpillar and lifted her with a brace. She'd stand for a few minutes then collapse. Even so, under our watchful eyes she calved, and her resourceful calf learned to suck with the cow down.

Other ranchers laughed at us and said we should shoot her because of the time we spent hauling water and lifting her. Maybe they were right. Three years earlier we'd lost a cow after working on her for a month before Phil finally had to shoot her. But we still insisted on giving this cow a chance. A month passed—and then one day she finally rose on her own. This time we kept the rifle in the truck.

Overworked ranchers rarely waste their time coddling anything. But whether large or small, wild or domestic, the creatures near Rosebud Creek find me looking out for them—even the birds.

When a finch, robin or quail, which eat at our various feeders, fly into a window, I rush out, pick up the stunned bird, and nestle it into the bunched cotton of a towel.

After breathless moments pass, the rescued bird often notices its companions swooping and chattering above. And then it soars upward and doesn't look back.

Scary Horses

In Izee they call it *cowboying*. It's one part of a rancher's job they all seem to love—riding horses while working cattle. The men, women, and even the tiniest children are all experts. But I'm convinced that danger follows horseback riding like the rain cloud follows Joe BTFSPLK in *Li'l Abne*r.

Such was the case one September, on the day before the opening of deer hunting season. With red streaks of dusk filling the sky, Phil and I set out to find five stray pairs (cows with calves) and bring them home before the hunters flooded the forest. Far out in front and determined to beat the dark, Phil sat astride Sandy, pushing him hard towards Wildcat Gulch. While Phil floated on Sandy's easy cantor, my horse Baldy, too ancient and fat, fairly slogged along behind. I slapped the saddle with each beat of his massive hooves as they pounded the packed dirt with a jarring rhythm.

The road, scarred with ruts and gouges from erosion, was a minefield of small boulders deposited from past waterspouts. Well-cultivated instincts told me that this speed (or *any* speed other than a leisurely stroll) over such a course was risky. But after successfully dodging a few divots and runnels, I felt gutsy and decided that maybe I *did* share DNA with Calamity Jane. We broke into a gallop.

Suddenly, Baldy's right front leg buckled, and he fell to his knees.

In an instant I knew that death, or at least paralysis, was a half-second away. If Baldy collapsed, he'd pitch me over his head and somersault on top of me. A panicky warning erupted from my throat. "Don't you go down! Don't you do it!" Clutching my hands to the saddle horn and squeezing my legs around his belly, I watched the earth come at my face. Then, miraculously, old Baldy used his momentum to heave himself up and recover his front feet, never missing a beat.

On yet another day, again in September, cattle needed to be gathered off Buck Creek's hills and pushed into the meadow. By then we'd bought an additional gelding, elderly and bombproof, called Whitey. I'd ridden him briefly in our driveway and found him gentle but a tad stubborn to neck rein. He trailed nicely on the well-worn path behind Phil and Sandy, so I took the time to appreciate the currant bushes, just beginning their transformation to red, and the musical burbling of the creek water trickling past the watercress.

Phil motioned for me to split off and begin surrounding the cows. As Whitey and I stepped off the path, he ran smack dab into a sage bush and stopped.

"That's okay, boy." I told him, rubbing his big neck. "My fault."

Minutes later, though I was guiding him, he overcorrected and tripped over a large piece of basalt. Then he walked off a small rock outcropping and almost tossed me. It was like a steering wheel with too much play.

I finally hollered out, "Phil, something's seriously wrong with Whitey!"

Phil looked back and watched us for a minute, then turned back around. Of course, Whitey looked perky. "Naw, he's fine."

"He isn't right, I'm telling you—"

"Kristy, for heaven's sake!" Phil barked impatiently. "*You* are the boss."

It seemed to me that throughout the day, Whitey persistently ignored my commands plunging into badger holes, charging barbed wire fences, and herding small juniper trees. So we were little help that day to a disgruntled Phil.

After a few days we took Whitey to get his teeth floated. The veterinarian looked in Whitey's eyes.

"Did you know this horse is almost totally blind?" he said. "I hope you weren't riding him—that could put someone in *real* danger."

Another episode happened on a crisp autumn evening while Phil (riding Sandy) and I (on Baldy) pushed a small cluster of cows up a steep hill. As the six pairs moved briskly in front of us, Phil nudged them straight up so we could take a shortcut over the top and then down to the highway below.

At the summit we found ourselves on a trail no wider than a garden hose, traveling along a rocky ridge. Each side had a sheer slope covered with loose topsoil. While Phil dropped off to the right to follow a couple of bunch-quitters, I gladly stayed on the narrow track behind the remaining five pairs. Before long, it had grown so dark that I could barely see the cows—a situation that prompted Baldy, who would normally stumble on an easy stroll across a new mown field in daylight, to step out like a Lipizzaner stallion. In fact, the darker it got, the faster he trotted.

"HOW 'BOUT LEAVING THESE COWS," I shouted down towards Phil, "AND COMING BACK IN THE DAYLIGHT?"

From down the hill came, "WE CAN'T STOP!"

With the steely confidence of a young stallion, Baldy tucked his rear-end and slid down the shale-littered slope. I knew I was going to die and braced myself for the end. But all of us—cattle, horses, and riders—made it intact to the highway. Then, almost immediately after we had put the tired animals through the gate, Baldy tripped on the smooth asphalt, probably to show me he still could.

Another time, Wisteria, one of our city pals, came to visit, and Phil decided that we'd take her on a horseback ride up the hills of Poison Draw to introduce her to our beloved eastern Oregon. The sun had two hours left when we started the trek. Phil rode the gelding, Dan, in front; Wisteria followed on Midget, an easy-going mare; and I, last in line, got the agreeable but arthritic Joe.

"Boy, this is great!" Wisteria said, twisting in the saddle to face me. The light glinted off her thick glasses. "You guys probably do this everyday. I sure would!"

I smiled confidently, slouching as I'd seen cowboys do. "Yeah, well, when we work the headstrong cows, sometimes we ride hard and fast nearly every day," I said, fibbing only slightly. Really, how was she to know, anyway? She flashed me a grin of happy awe with maybe a touch of hero worship.

At an unhurried pace, Phil guided us zigzagging up Airplane Ridge. Near the top, we turned south, angling down Poison Draw and traveling just under the ridge. Far below us, the old ranch house and barn looked like dollhouses. When we entered a high swale peppered with gnarly old junipers and old-growth pines, my horse, lagging yards behind the other two riders, grew unaccountably agitated. Unaware of the problem, Phil kept up a running commentary to Wisteria about local flora and fauna.

"Lots of grouse and Hungarian partridge up here..."

Joe ignored my reining and started dancing sideways.

"Oh, that's Indian Paintbrush..."

Then, not letting his arthritis slow him down, Joe's hind feet bucked up in the air, and I fell off. But the reins stayed clutched in my hands as he jerked at the end of them. In between Joe's scuffling, snatches of Phil's lecture floated back to me.

"Those are *elk* tracks as opposed to *deer*..."

Soon Phil and Wisteria popped over a small knoll, no doubt thinking I was still behind them. I didn't call to them because in Wisteria's eyes I was supposed to be an experienced ranch woman.

Suddenly, the explanation for Joe's problem became clear. Two wild horses rushed toward us from out of a dense stand of junipers. With heads arched and tails high, they looked ready to fight. Snorting and kicking, they whinnied their challenge. Frantic, I jumped up and down, wildly flailing one arm at them like a demented orchestra conductor while keeping a death grip on the reins. The sight must have flummoxed them because they stopped and stared.

"Hah!" I shouted. "Go!"

Then, slowly and slightly trembley, I started leading Joe. The two horses followed closely behind.

"Shoo!" I turned and yelled. "Bad horses! Get!"

Incredibly, they decided to peel off into the brush like a couple of wraiths sent to test my mettle. As if on cue and for the eerie effect, the sun slipped below the hill. Back up on old Joe, I gradually caught up with Phil and Wisteria, who were still deep in a chatty discussion.

"Bald eagles," Phil was saying, "Golden eagles, an occasional Kestrel—oh, and wild horses! Stallions will challenge geldings if a mare is nearby. It can be scary to come across them on horseback. But don't worry. There aren't any up here."

Night Checks

Another dead calf lay at our feet, the third this season. Its curly red and white fur sparkled from the March frost. Glazed eyes ringed with sweeping eyelashes stared at nothing. The mother, easy to spot with the afterbirth trailing from her vagina, trotted in agitation and circled the pasture. At least she was alive.

Since the start of calving season in February, Phil's decision to forgo the 3:00 a.m. check had cost us two calves and two paralyzed heifers out of our twenty-three first calvers. A downed cow often warranted a bullet. Rehabilitation ate up valuable time and the heifer usually would not recover on her own.

"I can just hear Jeff or Bard warning me," he said with a shrug. "'You're a one-man show, Phil, so you can't baby-sit 'em. If they don't calve on their own, get rid of 'em.'" Phil shook his head. "I hate to have them suffer or die, but I'm too exhausted to stay up all night."

Dammit—didn't he know from talking to those guys how this would be? Doing his regular chores and then rising every three hours at night to check heifers had made him goofy-tired. And it had made me grumpy. "I'll do it."

Did I really say that? After all, 3:00 a.m. was hunting time for vampires, werewolves, zombies or, worse yet, real-life slashers—not to mention cougars. Naturally, Phil was almost speechless with disbelief because he knew I was the biggest fraidy cat in the universe.

So at 3:00 I slammed off the alarm. Fat and Kallie, our two Australian Shepherds, came awake with a startled woof and launched themselves at the door ready for action. Luckily, just when those wily bed sirens called out with the temptation of cuddling spoon-fashion with Phil, the stark pictures of the lifeless heifers and their babies came sharply to mind. So Phil snored on as I quietly struggled into stiff overalls that easily covered a ratty turtleneck and long underwear. An old knit cap and Phil's thick wooly socks and Sorel pack boots completed the outfit.

My two furry-faced companions hopped up and down, eager to get out and load up. The dogs bumped each other shouldering out the door, where the temperature hovered close to twenty degrees, and bounded into the bed of the Toyota pickup.

After the midnight check, Phil had set a piece of plywood over the windshield to keep off the ice, so the window didn't need scraping, which would have afforded monsters a chance to nab me. Inside the cab, three-quarters of the seat was taken up by an old plastic milk crate filled with rusty coffee cans of nails, a couple of stiff grease rags, fencing pliers, hammers, calving chain, and several candy wrappers. The driver's seat offered a gaping wound of wire springs and pieces of foam rubber.

I slid in, sitting six inches below the surface of the seat, and noticed the pedals were too far away. Under the seat, the mud-encrusted scoot-up handle refused to budge. When I tossed Phil's walkie-talkie onto the dash, rattlesnake rattles, used batteries, and mystery keys tumbled to the floor into a two-inch layer of hay and dirt.

But the truck started okay, and the trip up the ice-glazed highway proved uneventful. Yet the obstacle that loomed ahead in the glare of the truck's one working headlight—opening, driving through, and closing the calving lot gate—gave predators ideal pouncing and devouring opportunities.

"Keep your eyes peeled, girls," I told the dogs. I wallowed up from the cratered seat and scampered over frozen mud ruts to the gate. This I followed with a nervous scan for anything loitering nearby with murderous intent, a quick unlatching, a hefty shove, and a jump back into the pickup. Same thing to close it.

The pickup bumped over frozen cow pies and badger holes while zigzagging through the living maze of cows, and the headlight lit up forty-six surprised eyes. Their noses puffed out cartoonish air like little steam engines. Some heifers lay chewing their refluxed cud while others stood over the morning's hay, plucking up leftovers missed earlier. One Angus cow used a stiff three-foot rye stem, just the right height, to rub with obvious pleasure the inside of her nostril. Boy, I thought, that's something they never showed on *Rawhide*. Neither did they show cattle cleaning their noses with their tongues, although it's probably not much different from dogs cleaning their rear-ends.

Suddenly the reason I left a comfy bed appeared. A white heifer, humped up in pain, back legs braced, oozed out a glossy calf head-first onto the ground. My hand flew for the walkie talkie where the quick press of a button would beep its mate next to Phil's ear. But then I stopped. Because the baby arrived okay and the caul burst as it came out, I chose to stick around and watch the new mom. The little heifer whipped around to see what had happened and spotted the squirming creature at her backend.

"AARRRGH!" She lifted her head like a wolf and bellowed repeatedly, pausing just long enough to roughly nose and butt the small intruder. Horrified, I lunged again to summon Phil, but then the heifer began licking the baby, starting at the head. The calf finally shook its head and sneezed.

"Er-er-er," the mama cooed, working her raspy tongue up and down the calf's body. Each sweep of the tongue excited the baby. The muffled cow language now changed to a question, maybe because the calf struggled to rise but continued to fall. "Hum-hum-hum?" the heifer murmured while the youngster tried to figure out its legs.

The amazing, or maybe even miraculous, thing was the success of the calf's next mission—finding food. As soon as its stick legs cooperated, the calf nuzzled under the heifer. Even as its mother moved around, the stubborn calf followed. When it finally, luckily bumped against the udder, a kind of madness took over. It latched onto a teat, punched its rubbery nose deep in the full udder to make its mother let down milk, and began slurping contentedly. Then, blessed peace. For all of us.

The night proved exhilarating. The stars twinkled, the Milky Way was a blurry swipe, and the crisp air held its breath in a muffled stillness. Fiends in this world as well as in the netherworld seemed to have granted me a pass through their domain. It was as if the early morning's good deed imparted limited immunity. Blissfully unaware of night terrors when we returned home, the dogs curled up on their sleeping pads and I in my bed, mission accomplished. Phil mumbled when he felt the bed move.

"Anything going on?" He asked, not really awake. "Problems?"

"Nope," I said. "But guess what hap—"

Phil snored. But that was okay. Let him sleep.

Close Call

Suddenly the chain saw stopped. For the last two hours, its screaming ebb and flow had ridden roughshod over the pattering rain as Phil cut junipers along Poison Creek. Now the silence made me jerk my nose out of a novel, uneasiness pricking my consciousness. Sitting in the Chevy pickup a hundred yards down a nearly vertical slope, I waited for Phil, who had instructed me to let him fall a few trees before bringing the gas and oil up to him. But the absence of his noisy work triggered an awakening.

Cranking down the fogged-up window, I listened hard. Sounds of drippy water and panting animals drifted in. Panting animals? Our dogs—Fat and Kallie, who were *always* with Phil—now lay near the truck. No longer attempting to curb my jump-the-gun imagination, I bound out of the pickup, scaring the pups as I let out a fishwife holler up the mountain. "PHIL!"

A tiny sound came back, causing the dogs' ears to shoot forward. Both fixed their eyes uphill. My stomach lurched.

I rapidly scanned the juniper-littered area where Phil had already cut down twenty or more trees.

"PHIL! WHERE ARE YOU?"

Another small squeak floated down, the sound resembling the Tin Man before Scarecrow squirted oil in his joints. Fat and Kallie heard it and took off up a mucky, pebbly trail. I followed, yelling with each footstep. Then, gulping for air, I paused. A bushy maze of newly-cut trees blocked the view.

Finally, close by, a gasping plea—"Here-Hurry."

Phil's voice wafted from a sawn tree lying uphill rather than pointing down like the others. My heart galloping, I plunged to my knees, scooting in as far as possible under the snarled mass of thick branches and frantically searched for him.

"Honey! Phil! Are you under here?"

I wiggled in deeper, ignoring the scratch of juniper needles until I finally found him—facing downhill and lying beneath a four-inch-wide branch of a thirty-foot juniper with a trunk three feet thick. The limb leaned across Phil's right side, wedging him against the rocky topsoil. He could barely turn his head, and mud crusted his mouth. Nearby, his Homelite chainsaw lay partially covered by another thick limb, as though Phil had flung it as he'd darted sideways from the tumbling tree.

"Quick-crushing-me." His words came with small, jerking breaths.

How was I going to get him out? It seemed impossible.

"I have to get help!"

"DON'T! I-won't-make-it."

His breathing grew ragged. With growing despair I realized we needed someone, maybe lots of someones, to get Phil out from under the tree. But no one knew where we were.

Then it occurred to me that maybe I could lift the branch like the old woman who had miraculously hoisted the car that had rolled onto her grandchild. So I tried. It didn't budge. Stupid *National Enquirer*!

After a long, long moment Phil whispered, "Other-saw-in-truck."

I took off, sliding and scooting down to the truck with the dogs scampering playfully behind, thinking it was a new game. I grabbed the smaller saw and started back. But after twenty feet my breath was gone, and a wicked stitch knifed my side. Rage bubbled inside me. This is great, just great! Phil is fighting to stay alive, and I can't get a breath after walking a hundred feet up the damn hill! I trudged on.

"I'VE GOT IT!" I shouted as soon as I got near his tree.

Gut-wrenching silence.

Then, slowly, his small wheezing voice: "Turn-it-on. Pull-cord."

Over and over again I tried. Not a cough or a hiccup erupted from that worthless saw.

"Oil-gas."

"What? Oh. In the truck." I skittered all the way down, trying not to think bad thoughts. We'd been together since we were teenagers. Moving to the ranch, far from our families, we depended only on each other. So far, it had always turned out all right. Just like it would today.

On the way back to Phil, it was the same story. Pain in my side. Start and stop. Babies were conceived, born, and died of old age during my ascent.

When at last I reach his side, Phil explained in a faltering voice how to put in the gas and oil. After a couple of strong jerks, the small saw started. Revving it high, I somehow managed to cut out two or three little branches, clearing a small space near Phil. Then as I sliced into a massive branch, the gash closed on the saw's bar and pinched the chain to a stop. "CRAP, CRAP, CRAP!"

Thankfully, Phil kept a clear head, even while the weight of the tree pressed into his body. "Try-big-one."

I jimmied the unwieldy saw with its thirty-two inch bar away from the tangled boughs and tried hoisting it clear. Not a chance. "Now can I get help?"

"NO! Get-the-hydraulic-jack."

His voice conveyed pain, but now terror had crept in, too, and adrenaline surged through me. About time. "No problem. Hang on." I started to shiver but tried for a light tone. "Don't panic, honey!"

I scrambled recklessly down the mountain, slammed into the truck bed, jumped in like an Olympic pole-vaulter, and unearthed the thirty-pound jack from beneath pieces of soppy ranch debris. Then, grunting and cussing, I shifted its four-foot-long bulk over the edge of the tailgate and onto the ground, gouging out a small crater. In lurching stages I dragged it up the hill, the jack plowing out a tiny San Andreas Fault behind me while Fat and Kallie mischievously nipped at it. Along the way it collected sagebrush, baby junipers, and small boulders, fashioning a poor man's Christmas tree. Previous trips had taken ten minutes whereas this one clocked twenty.

When my head finally poked into Phil's tree prison, happiness washed over his dirty face. "Thought-you'd-gone," he croaked, so softly I could hardly hear him. He had used his free arm to grub out a spot below the branch, then wedged his upright forearm under it to keep the tree from crushing him. "The-jack?" I pushed it toward him. "Noooo," he said, groaning. "Smaller-behind-seat."

With rain and sweat washing my face, I blundered back down the divoted path. Exhausted, Fat and Kallie stayed behind.

This jack weighed maybe an eighth of what the big one did, so I scuttled it up to Phil, carrying it one-handed. It fit perfectly under the branch. As I pumped the short handle, Phil anxiously watched the wood lift. When the pressure on him finally eased, he wiggled.

"Chop-little-ax."

I snatched the ax off the ground and chopped the branch between the jack and the trunk. Fragrant pieces of juniper flew in the air until it finally snapped. Gripping Phil hard, I dragged him as he crawled away from the tree.

Once in the open, he leaned against me and trembled uncontrollably. Then he lifted his face to the sky to savor the cooling mist. "I've learned three things," he said, speaking faintly. "Always saw the lower branches first to give an escape route, cut a wedge so the tree falls right, and never—ever—do this alone."

Much later, a doctor's examination would reveal that Phil had bruised and cracked ribs and some minor nerve damage. But for now we held each other fiercely, unwilling to break apart, murmuring words of love, thankfulness, and joy. Then we began the trip back down to the truck. Together.

Just Dogs

At the beginning of our life on the ranch, we were lousy dog owners. Our pets didn't get fresh biscuits, new chew-toys, or a place at the foot of our bed. Instead, they lay on dirty blankets piled on an icy porch, or in the back of a pickup filled with hay hooks and barbed wire. After all, they were just dogs.

As time went by, however, their uncomplicated personalities and their desire to please inspired us to do better, and we learned something new from each dog. It began with our Huskies.

It had been unfair to bring this Alaskan breed, Belle and her daughter Whitewater, into cow country because they roamed and ended up killing the chickens of our closest neighbor, the Andersons. Instead of building a fence to keep the Huskies in, we handed them over to a dog musher in Bend. (It was also an unpardonable excuse for us to get a "cow" dog). But before we shuffled them off, Belle had ten puppies by the Anderson's Australian Shepherd. The one we kept, probably because he was part cow dog, was epileptic and needed daily medication to curtail the debilitating seizures. In spite of that, he radiated joyfulness. We called him Rooster.

One day as I sat on the kitchen floor, wallowing in grumpiness for a reason I can't recall, Rooster suddenly bounded into the room and plunked down in front of me, wanting to play. He tried the dog stare on me, half-challenging, half-guilt-inducing. After getting no response, he rolled over and over like a trained circus dog. Making sure I was paying attention, he kept at it until I giggled. Then, satisfied, he launched into my arms and covered my face with slurpy kisses.

Then one day while we were in town, a hired hand of my dad's let Rooster eat poisoned squirrels. Rooster crawled under dad's porch, hiding in pain and dying. The man quit, but not before telling us he'd heard Rooster crying. We didn't find our dead pup until a month later.

After this special dog, we got a pure Australian Shepherd, Rooster II, from Sheehan's dogs. When Rooster II was old enough to come along on cattle drives, the neighbors' older male dogs would jump him from behind, so we decided to stop taking him until he grew a little. But soon after reaching his first birthday, he was hit while crossing the highway in front of our house. (This was during our *Who cares where the dog is?* days). The vet said Rooster II's broken pelvis would heal slowly.

When he had mended enough, we let him jog in front of the pickup as we drove the two miles up Poison Draw. The workouts agreed with him. Soon he was racing like a Greyhound and muscling up like a boxer. He was so fast and fit that he once jumped over a coiled rattler, clearing it by a foot as the snake struck. On the next cattle drive, Rooster II established his dominance over the other dogs with some swift bites on their ears and a crunch or two on their legs.

But one day when we had to leave the ranch for what turned out to be three months, we left him in the care of neighbors. When we returned he was gone. He deserved a better deal than the one he got from us. After this abandonment, an unforgivable mistake on our part, it was a while before we felt we had earned the right to own another dog.

When we finally brought dogs back into our lives, three of them lived past fifteen years, eventually dying of old age. Oddly, all three also suffered rattlesnake's bites and survived.

Two of these, Kallie and Fat—mother and daughter, both Aussies—were my running buddies their whole lives and worked cattle, too. These dogs endured feeding cows in winter snowstorms and long cattle drives in summer heat. They accompanied me as we ran past (and were sometimes chased by) rattlesnakes, porcupines, badgers, and coyotes.

One such run came during a gnats-in-your-teeth morning in May. While my

Nikes slapped along the dirt path towards the one-and-a-half-mile mark, Fat snuffled out a hot trail in the high-grassed meadow nearby, and Kallie pattered alongside. Not keen to take my eyes off the knobby road, my peripheral vision registered Fat scaring up a coyote. She chased it leisurely uphill, and because coyotes always shift into overdrive, this one's dawdling just didn't make sense.

When Kallie and I reached the border fence and started back, I was sure Fat would join us as soon as the scent grew cold. But as yards of hardpan passed beneath my strides, a movie reel seemed to play in my head, bringing up the flash-card image of Fat's playmate: Its tail was too long and skinny for a coyote, its movement too sinewy. The recognition button from National Geographic TV programs flicked on. The puzzle fell into place. With a quarter-mile left to the safety of our yard, I knew Fat's coyote was actually a cougar.

Suddenly I imagined her flanks ripped with claw marks, her bloody intestines dragging behind her. But before I experienced full-blown panic, Fat rejoined us for the last yards of the run. And she was in one piece. (Damn imagination!) Nevertheless, a cougar had been hiding in the tall grass, and I was thankful to have had the dogs with me.

The third long-lived dog, Magic, had her world turned upside down when she had to leave her original family at the age of six and join ours, including Fat and Kallie. But Magic possessed a heart that was willing to love and trust all over again. When she first arrived, the thirty-five-pound Fat challenged Magic, who was half-German Shepherd, half-Airedale, and weighed more than sixty-five solid pounds. To her credit, she simply stood over Fat, letting her know it was wise to back down. Fat did. Magic never laid tooth or claw on either dog; instead, she chose to express her might through tender persuasion.

During one cattle drive through the forest, for example, Magic jumped a porcupine that filled her face and mouth with quills. Because we had to keep the cattle moving, we couldn't help her until hours later that evening, when we pulled out at least fifty quills. During this agony she demonstrated more resiliency than many humans we've known.

Yet up to this point, Magic, as well as all our other dogs, slept either outside or on the porch, even in frigid weather. What changed that was Billie, a hybrid composed of English Shepherd, Airedale, Aussie, and Catahoula Hound. Billie was different. As a pup, she'd lie on her back and watch us upside down for a long time, or she'd edge into our laps during breaks on cattle drives, or when we were sitting on the deck or even in vehicles. She snored when she slept and trilled when she was happy.

When she was five months old, we boarded her at the vet's kennel for four days. When I went to pick her up and the vet's assistant spoke harshly to her, Billie slumped as if struck. On the trip home she wouldn't come to the front seat but only stared out the window. Finally, I stopped the car. After much coaxing she finally came forward. I hugged her and she stiffened. It took five minutes of speaking softly before Billie looked me in the eye and snuggled into my lap. That evening the couch became her bed.

Six months later, Billie died on the highway in front of our house—still no fence—and her death made us question our sense of right and wrong when dealing with our dogs. It also made us appreciate the traits that defined them: the Huskies' lonesome howls, Rooster I's healing acrobatics, Rooster II's stoicism, Fat and Kallie's companionship and courage, and Magic's resolve to fit in and be loved.

Today our two dogs, Dollie, a Border Collie, and Rizzo, a Carter dog, sleep on pillows in our bedroom, munch dog biscuits, share squeaky toys, and sit on the couch with us to watch movies in the evening. A fence surrounds the house. They still ride in the back of old pickups—cleaned of hooks and wire—but only because that's what they prefer. After all, they are just dogs.

Dad's Death

In the summer of 1977, I walked into Dad's living room at the ranch just as he stuck a hypodermic needle into his arm and pushed the plunger. "Dad! What *is* that?"

"'S okay, honey," he slurred. "Jus' helps the pain caused by tha' old plane wreck. Doctor sen' some home with me." His head flopped back against the leather chair. He was asleep.

No, it wasn't okay. And there never had been a plane wreck. He forgot I knew the truth. Without any remorse, I ransacked his stuff. Tiny vials tumbled out of the Alta Bates Hospital bag. The labels all said *Morphine*. So now Dad was hooked on morphine as well as alcohol. To neighbors he had fabricated stories about his pre-Izee history to justify his addictions. Surprisingly, some defended him even when told the truth.

"C'mon," one neighbor would say, "he drinks because he bombed that Korean orphanage."

"Dad wasn't in Korea," I'd say. "He joined the navy in 1944 at seventeen. After a month in the brig he called his mom to get him out."

"No way! He just didn't tell you."

Another would insist, "It's the years of rodeoing that got him drinking."

"He's never ridden a bucking horse in his life." I said to the millionth person giving me that *you-ungrateful-whelp* look.

"For shame, doubting your father." Disapproval clouded his face. "You live on his ranch, don't you?"

Meanwhile whenever Dad ran out of liquor, the Izee ranchers found him on their doorsteps at all hours hoping to score some whiskey. So late one night, ringing jarred us awake.

"WHASSAT?" Phil screamed after a knuckle-crunching day repairing fence. "SPEAK, DAMMIT!"

"You have to pick up the phone first," I said, my head under the pillow. "That's the way it works." He grabbed the receiver.

"Phil?" Jeff Gallagher said on the other end. "Paul tipped over his Jeep in the ditch next to my driveway. He's one drunk dweezle. I explained there's no liquor here so he offered a two-inch wad of hundreds if I'd drive him to town. Nope, I said. It's after midnight and nothin's open. Then he passed out. I'll bring him on home for you."

Jeff got off easy that night. When it came to morphine, Dad hated giving himself a shot, so he often persuaded neighbors to do it. As an excuse, he invented a muscle twitch over his heart. Each performance merited an Oscar.

"Yeah. I did it," said Rafe from the Izee Ranch. "His chest was wiggling around like a couple of squirrels battling over an acorn. He'd gasp and gurgle. I felt like a damn fool, but I thought what if it's *really* a heart attack?"

During these morphine episodes, Dad neglected ranch business. He ignored a county mandate ordering him to spray his Whitetop, an invasive weed that spreads to other ranches. The county sprayed for him, but Dad disregarded the bill. Consequently, they slapped a lien on the ranch, and the original owner took steps to foreclose. Soon the ranch was scheduled for auction at a sheriff's sale on the courthouse steps.

Making it worse, Dad's health was failing. Though only fifty, he shuffled like an eighty-year-old. At six foot two, he now weighed only one hundred and seventy.

"Dad," I said, "please get help or you'll die."

He raised his head and stared at me with eyes as blue as the Izee sky. "I'll be okay, princess."

The next morning he was hitching a ride on someone's plane back to California and the morphine. After a couple days, he called from San Francisco.

"Sweetheart," he said. "Did you hear Elvis died of a drug overdose?" He sounded worn-out.

"I heard. *Please* come home. You need to rest."

"Working on a deal—then I'll be home. See you soon, honey."

That was the last time I heard my father's voice.

In the back of my mind hovered a growing uneasiness. Miles of fence needed fixing, and we were late moving Dad's cattle into the last forest pasture. Then in the first week of September came another phone call.

"Paul Timm, admitted for heart problems, is my patient at Alta Bates Hospital here in San Francisco," said an official-sounding voice. "I'm sorry to tell you he choked on his breakfast this morning, asphyxiated, and lapsed into a coma. He's critical, and you may want to come down"

Within hours I was rushing south with my half-sister Paige. We drove through the night for nine hours straight. But twenty minutes before we arrived, Dad died. The autopsy revealed a strong, whole heart but a diseased liver.

The next few days blurred. Dad's ashes arrived in the mail. While thunderheads loomed above the old pioneer cemetery on Dad's ranch, Phil and my brother-in-law Jim dug the hole for his remains. Rain threatened, but the air was still. As they placed the container into the ground, coyotes on three ridges howled, their sopranos ricocheting off the hills.

Later, a chilly September breeze pushed against cowboy hats and hair-sprayed coifs. Fifty or sixty souls, some related but most not, gathered around the freshly-dug earth. With a quivering voice, I sang a Psalm and strummed the guitar. Phil sang along. Angus, Dad's first Izee friend, scattered rosebuds onto the grave. The air turned icy, and Phil's father put his coat around my shoulders. Because my grandmother was there, I struggled with platitudes rather than give the earthy or humorous tribute my Dad would have loved ("Secret lover of Marilyn Monroe. Funnier than Bob Hope. More handsome than Tom Selleck. Taught Sinatra to croon)."

"WHUT—IS—SHE—SAYIN'?" bellowed Web Snively, an Izee rancher older than the juniper he stood under. "AN' WHO *IS* SHE, ANYHOW?"

"Shush, Web," whispered his wife, Matilda. They huddled together on the fringes of the Izee crowd.

"BUT AH JEST CAN'T HEER. SHE NEEDS TO SPEAK UP. WHAT'S THE GOOD O' COMIN' IF A MAN CAIN'T HEER?"

Before I could finish the eulogy, I spotted Amy Gallagher nearby, sobbing. Next to her, my quadriplegic uncle cowered in his wheelchair, his eyes showing panic while a man he obviously didn't know fawned all over him. "I laid Paul's *carpet*," said the stranger, sopping drunk. "He was a wunerful man, you know?"

Then an autumn shower ended the service early, and we hurried to the ranch house, which filled quickly. The ladies from church had laid out every kind of comfort food ever invented, especially for wakes, but one church matron was doing her best to fend off the drunken carpet-guy.

"You don' unerstan'," he said. "I PUT DOWN THIS HERE RUG." Then he burst into tears and had to be led out to his car.

Eleven relatives on my mother's side—except for the paralyzed uncle who was telling someone how nice it was that Dad had such a caring carpet man—started singing while doing the bunny-hop around the house, while the Izee folks stared open mouthed at them. But Dad would have approved of his wake's irreverence, unruliness and, most of all, its goofiness.

Overwhelmed by memories, I slipped outside for privacy.

He was my childhood hero. The man who sang Sinatra's "The Lady is a Tramp" on elevators filled with strangers. Who loved his three-year-old standing beside him on the car seat, hugging his neck as he drove. Who taught his daughter to be silly enough to fit in at school. I'd miss that father. The brilliant, funny one. The man who, after escaping from a mental hospital, bought a ranch.

Now I worried what was going to happen to that ranch—and there was *plenty* to worry about. With Dad's estate more than a half-million dollars in debt, the I.R.S. bearing down on ten year's of unpaid taxes, and the ranch on the auction block, Phil and I found ourselves as two ex-hippies with twenty dollars in our checking account and zero savings. That's when Phil's dad came to the rescue.

Pop loved the ranch. But Phil and I hadn't realized the depth of his passion until he borrowed on his investment properties to purchase it. His bid at the auction was the highest. To help make the payments, he leased the four thousand acres to an Izee neighbor, Ernst Hoffsted, for ten years. The ranch stayed in the family, and we didn't have to move away. But because Pop couldn't afford to pay us for our work, we did everything we could to survive and stay on the ranch.

During this time, Phil and I found occasional jobs with the neighbors. We branded, fixed fence, moved and gathered cattle. Because we didn't get paid much, we applied for cost-share help for conservation projects on the ranch, such as thinning junipers, developing springs, and building fences. We also cut firewood and hauled it to town to sell, logged a small stand of timber, and did some contract thinning on the Malheur National Forest; Phil sometimes helped the Sheehans hay, or piled brush on logging and thinning sites for the Hoffsteds. In addition, we continued doing leather work, sending it to galleries and attending art fairs to sell it.

At the end of the ten-year lease, Pop sold his house and three acres in Lake Oswego to pay off the ranch. With the property finally free and clear, Phil persuaded his dad to buy ten pregnant cows to begin our herd, and the St. Clairs were once again in the cow business.

Even though that was more than thirty years ago, we're still here. Today I thrive in wide-open spaces where my closest neighbor is a mile away, where cows moo for their calves, elk graze on the hay meadow, cougars pass in the night, and coyotes sing us to sleep here in Izee—the perfect home, it seems to me, for an accidental cowgirl.

About the Author

Kristy St. Clair

Although a fourth generation Californian on her mother's side, Kristy came to Oregon when she was fourteen. At eighteen, she married Phil St. Clair, the boy she believed would put up with her and her odd family, and in the 1960's they began careers in Portland as hippie leather craftsmen and sandal makers in a craft gallery called The Red Balloon. Surrounded by older artists from the Beat Generation, the couple's apprenticeship was beyond price, with painters, potters, sculptors, and writers serving as their mentors. Phil and Kristy sold their work at juried, high end art-and-craft show, and participated in group shows as well as two-man and one-man gallery shows.

Then one gloomy Portland day when she was twenty-four, Kristy's father suggested they visit his newly acquired cattle ranch east of the Cascades. Phil, a native western Oregonian with the gills required to survive the drizzle, was puzzled at Kristy's need to find the sun. But after just one ranch visit, the two packed their leather awls, rolled up their latigo cowhides, and headed to where the cows still wore their skins. They never looked back.

For the last three decades, instead of sipping Pinot Noir at gallery openings they got to hunker sweat-soaked alongside streams after cattle drives, look down from a ridge on horseback and watch bull elk fuss at his harem, and get splattered with afterbirth while hauling a sluggish calf out from its mother's back end. Along the way, Kristy acquired a university degree at Eastern Oregon University while at the same time driving Phil crazy helping him on the ranch. At some point, she realized writing was the best way to let readers know about Izee as well as the people who have influenced her life.

Kristy's articles have appeared in Cowboy Magazine ("Cowboying in Eastern Oregon," summer 2003), RANGE Magazine, ("The Indomitable Spirit of Kate Jordan," fall 2004), RANGE Magazine ("Buckaroo Wisdom," spring 2004), American Western Ezine ("Corral Savvy," 2003), Hallowzine ("Hunting Fate," 2002), and the Blue Mountain Eagle ("The Hunting," 2001).